Indiana Bicycle Trails
& selected Kentucky Trails

An
American Bike Trails
Publication

Indiana Bicycle Trails
& selected Kentucky Trails

Published by American Bike Trails

Copyright 2007 by American Bike Trails

All Rights Reserved. Reproduction of any part of this book in any form without written permission is prohibited.

Created by   Ray Hoven

Illustrated & Designed by   Mary C. Rumpsa

American Bike Trails assumes no responsibility or liability for any person or entity with respect to injury or damage caused either directly or indirectly by the information contained in this book.

Table of Contents

Trail Name	Page No.
How To Use This Book	6
Bicycle Safety	7
Health Hazards	10
Explanation of Geological Terms	12
Riding Tips	14
Explanation of Symbols	15

Indiana

Trail Name	Page No.
Indiana & Kentucky Sectionals	16
Northern Indiana	18
Bluhm County Park	20
Bonneyville Mill County Park	22
East Race Riverwalk	24
France Park	26
J.B. Franke Park	28
Kekionga Trail–Huntington Lake Recreation Area	30
Lake City Greenway	32
Nickel Plate Trail	35
Northwest Indiana Regional Bikeways	38
Pennsy Greenway	38
Iron Horse Heritage Trail	38
Veterans Memorial Trail	39
Erie Lackawanna Trail	40
Oak Savannah Trail	42
Prairie Duneland Trail	44
Calumet Trail	46
Outback Trail	48
Ox Bow County Park	50
Pumpkinvine Nature Trail	52
Rivergreenway	54
Rum Village Annex	58
Winona Lake Trail	60
Central Indiana	62

Table of Contents (continued)

Trail Name	Page No.
Indianapolis Greenways	64
Cardinal Greenway	66
Central Canal Towpath	68
Delphi Historic Trails	70
Eagle Creek Trail	72
Fall Creek Trail	74
Monon Trail & Monon Greenway	76
Owen-Putnam State Forest	80
Pleasant Run Trail	82
Pogue's Run Trail	84
Sugar Creek Community Trail	86
Town Run Trail Park	88
Westwood Park	90
White River Wapahani Trail	92
Southern Indiana	94
Birdseye Trail (Hoosier National Forest)	96
Bloomington's Trails	98
Bloomington Rail-Trail	98
Clear Creek Rail-Trail	98
Jackson Creek Trail	98
B-Line Trail	98
Bloomington's Trails	100
Brown County State Park	102
Clark State Forest	104
Ferdinand State Forest	106
German Ridge Recreation Area	108
Gnaw Bone Camp	110
Hickory Ridge Recreation Area	112
Hoosier National Forest	114
Jackson-Washington State Forest	116
Lick Creek Trail	118
Linton Conservation Club	120
Martin State Forest	122

Trail Name	Page No.
Mogan Ridge Trail West	124
Nebo Ridge Trail	126
Ogala Trail	128
Oriole Trails – West & East	131
Shirley Creek Trail	134
Springs Valley Trail	136
Starve Hollow State Recreation Area	138
Tipsaw Lake Trail	140
Wapehani Mountain Bike Park	142
Yellow Banks Recreation Area	144
Youngs Creek Trail	146
Explanation of Symbols	149

Kentucky

Selected Kentucky Trails	150
Ben Hawes State Park	152
Briar Hill (Oldham County Park)	154
Canal Loop	156
Capital View Trails	158
Cherokee Park	160
Fort Duffield	162
General Butler State Park (Fossil Trail)	164
Green River State Park	166
Louisville Riverwalk Trail	168
North South Trail	172
Otter Creek Park	174
Tower Park	176

Indexes

Trail Index	178
Surfaced Trails	180
Mountain Bike Trails	181
City to Trail Index	183
County to Trail Index	186
Bicycle Components & Tips	188

How To Use This Book

This book provides a comprehensive, easy-to use reference to the many off-road trails throughout Indiana & Kentucky. It contains over 70 detailed trails maps. The book is organized by geographical sections: Northern Indiana, Central Indiana, Southern Indiana, central & western Kentucky. Each section begins with a map of that section showing trail locations together with a reference listing of trails within the section. The back of the book provides indexes in alphabetical sequence of all the trails illustrated, plus separate listings by leisure and mountain biking, and cross references by city to trail and county to trail. The trail maps include such helpful features as locations and access, trail facilities, and nearby communities.

Terms Used

Length		Expressed in miles one way. Round trip mileage is normally indicated for loops.
Effort Levels	Easy	Physical exertion is not strenuous. Climbs and descents as well as technical obstacles are more minimal. Recommended for beginners.
	Moderate	Physical exertion is not excessive. Climbs and descents can be challenging. Expect some technical obstacles.
	Difficult	Physical exertion is demanding. Climbs and descents require good riding skills. Trail surface may be sandy, loose rock, soft or wet.
Directions		Describes by way of directions and distances, how to get to the trail areas from roads and nearby communities.
Map		Illustrative representation of a geographic area, such as a state, section, forest, park or trail complex.
DNR		Department of Natural Resources
DOT		Department of Transportation

Types of Biking

Mountain	Fat-tired bikes are recommended. Ride may be generally flat but then with a soft, rocky or wet surface.
Leisure	Off-road gentle ride. Surface is generally paved or screened.
Tour	Riding on roads with motorized traffic or on road shoulders.

Bicycle Safety

Bicycling offers many rewards, among them a physically fit body and a pleasant means of transportation. But the sport has its hazards, which can lead to serious accidents and injuries. We have provided rules, facts and tips that can help minimize the dangers of bicycling while you're having fun.

Choose The Right Bicycle

Adults and children should ride bicycles with frames small enough to be straddled easily with both feet flat on the ground, and with handlebars that can be easily reached with elbows bent. Oversize bikes make it difficult to ride comfortably and maintain control. Likewise, don't buy a large bike for a child to grow into--smaller is safer.

Learn To Ride The Safe Way

When learning to ride a bike, let a little air out of the tires, and practice steering and balancing by "scootering" around with both feet on the ground and the seat as low as possible. The "fly-or-fall" method-where someone runs alongside the bicycle and then lets go-can result in injuries.

Training wheels don't work, since the rider can't learn to balance until the wheels come of. They can be used with a timid rider, but the child still will have to learn to ride without them. Once the rider can balance and pedal (without training wheels), raise the seat so that the rider's leg is almost straight at the bottom of the pedal stroke.

Children seldom appreciate the dangers and hazards of city cycling. Make sure they understand the traffic laws before letting them onto the road.

Use This Important Equipment

Headlight A working headlight and rear reflector are required for night riding in some states. Side reflectors do not make the rider visible to drivers on cross streets.

Safety seat for children under 40 lbs. Make sure the seat is mounted firmly over the rear wheel of the bike, and does not wobble when going downhill at high speed. Make sure the child will not slide down while riding. The carrier should also have a device to keep the child's feet from getting into the spokes.

Package rack Racks are inexpensive, and they let the rider steer with both hands and keep packages out of the spokes.

Bicycle Safety (continued)

Beware Of Dangerous Practices

Never ride against traffic. Failure to observe this rule causes the majority of car-bicycle collisions. Motorists can't always avoid the maneuvers of a wrong-way rider since the car and bike move toward each other very quickly.

Never make a left turn from the right lane.

Never pass through an intersection at full speed.

Never ignore stop light or stop signs.

Never enter traffic suddenly from a driveway or sidewalk. This rule is particularly important when the rider is a child, who is more difficult for a motorist to see.

Don't wear headphones that make it hard to hear and quickly respond to traffic.

Don't carry passengers on a bike. The only exception is a child under 40 lbs. who is buckled into an approved bike safety seat and wears a helmet as required by law.

Passenger trailers can be safe and fun. Be aware, though, that a trailer makes the bike much longer and requires careful control. Passengers must wear helmets.

Get A Bike That Works With You

Skilled riders who use their bikes often for exercise or transport should consider buying multi-geared bikes, which increase efficiency while minimizing stress on the body. (These bikes may not be appropriate for young or unskilled riders, who may concentrate more on the gears than on the road.) The goal is to keep the pedals turning at a rate of 60-90 RPM. Using the higher gears while pedaling slowly is hard on the knees, and is slower and more tiring than the efficient pedaling on the experienced cyclist. Have a safe trip!

What To Look For In A Bicycle Helmet

We endorse these guidelines for bicycle helmets recommended by the American Academy of Pediatrics:

The helmet should meet the voluntary testing standards of one of these two groups: American National Standards Institute (ANSI) OR Snell Memorial Foundation. Look for a sticker on the inside of the helmet.

1.) Select the right size. Find one that fits comfortably and doesn't pinch.

2.) Buy a helmet with a durable outer shell and a polystyrene liner. Be sure it allows adequate ventilation.

3.) Use the adjustable foam pads to ensure a proper fit at the front, back and sides.

4.) Adjust the strap for a snug fit. The helmet should cover the top of your forehead and not rock side to side or back and forth with the chain strap in place.

5.) Replace your helmet if it is involved in an accident.

Emergency Toolkit

When venturing out on bicycle tours, it is always smart to take along equipment to help make roadside adjustments and repairs. It is not necessary for every member of your group to carry a complete set of equipment, but make sure someone in your group brings along the equipment listed below:

1.) Standard or slotted screwdriver
2.) Phillips screwdriver
3.) 6" or 8" adjustable wrench
4.) Small pliers
5.) Spoke adjuster
6.) Tire pressure gauge
7.) Portable tire pump
8.) Spare innertube
9.) Tire-changing lugs

A Few Other Things

When embarking on a extended bike ride, it is important to give your bike a pre-ride check. To ensure that your bike is in premium condition, go over the bike's mechanisms, checking for any mechanical problems. It's best to catch these at home, and not when they occur "on the road." If you run into a problem that you can't fix yourself, you should check your local yellow pages for a professional bike mechanic.

When you are planning a longer trip, be sure to consider your own abilities and limitations, as well as those of any companions who may be riding with you. In general, you can ride about three times the length (time-wise) as your average training ride. If you have a regular cycling routine, this is a good basis by which to figure the maximum distance you can handle.

Finally, be aware of the weather. Bring plenty of sunblock for clear days, and rain gear for the rainy one. Rain can make some rides miserable, in addition to making it difficult to hear other traffic. Winds can blow up sand, and greatly increase the difficulty of a trail.

Trail Courtesy & Common Sense

1.) Stay on designated trails.

2.) Bicyclists use the right side of the trail (Walkers use the left side of the trail).

3.) Bicyclists should only pass slower users on the left side of the trail; use your voice to warn others when you need to pass.

4.) Get off to the side of the trail if you need to stop.

5.) Bicyclists should yield to all other users.

6.) Do not use alcohol or drugs while on the trail.

7.) Do not litter.

8.) Do not trespass onto adjacent land.

9.) Do not wear headphones while using the trail.

Health Hazards

Hypothermia

Hypothermia is a condition where the core body temperature falls below 90 degrees. This may cause death.

Mild hypothermia

1. Symptoms
   a. Pronounced shivering
   b. Loss of physical coordination
   c. Thinking becomes cloudy
2. Causes
   a. Cold, wet, loss of body heat, wind
3. Treatment
   a. Prevent further heat loss, get out of wet clothing and out of wind. Replace wet clothing with dry.
   b. Help body generate more heat. Refuel with high-energy foods and a hot drink, get moving around, light exercise, or external heat.

Severe hypothermia

1. Symptoms
   a. Shivering stops, pulse and respiration slows down, speech becomes incoherent.
2. Treatment
   a. Get help immediately.
   b. Don't give food or water.
   c. Don't try to rewarm the victim in the field.
   d. A buildup of toxic wastes and tactic acid accumulates in the blood in the body's extremities. Movement or rough handling will cause a flow of the blood from the extremities to the heart. This polluted blood can send the heart into ventricular fibrillations (heart attack). This may result in death.
   e. Wrap victim in several sleeping bags and insulate from the ground.

Frostbite
Symptoms of frostbite may include red skin with white blotches due to lack of circulation. Rewarm body part gently. Do not immerse in hot water or rub to restore circulation, as both will destroy skin cell.

Heat Exhaustion
Cool, pale, and moist skin, heavy sweating, headache, nausea, dizziness and vomiting. Body temperature nearly normal.

Treatment: Have victim lie in the coolest place available – on back with feet raised. Rub body gently with cool, wet cloth. Give person glass of water every 15 minutes if conscious and can tolerate it. Call for emergency medical assistance.

Heat Stroke
Hot, red skin, shock or unconsciousness; high body temperature.

Treatment: Treat as a life-threatening emergency. Call for emergency medical assistance immediately. Cool victim by any means possible. Cool bath, pour cool water over body, or wrap wet sheets around body. Give nothing by mouth.

Explanation of Geological Terms

Bog An acidic wetland that is fed by rainwater and is characterized by open water with a floating mat of vegetation (e.g. sedges, mosses, tamarack) that will often bounce if you jump on it.

Bluff A high steep bank with a broad, flat, or rounded front.

Canyon A deep, narrow valley with precipitous sides, often with a stream flowing through it.

Fen An alkaline wetland that is fed by ground water and is often seen as a wet meadow and characterized by plants like Grass or Parnasis and sedges that grow in alkaline water.

Forest A vegetative community dominated by trees and many containing understory layers of smaller trees, shorter shrubs and an herbaceous layers at the ground.

Grove A small wooded area without underbrush, such as a picnic area.

Herb A seed producing annual, biennial, or perennial that does not develop persistent woody tissue but dies down at the end of a growing season.

Karst An irregular limestone region with sinks, underground streams, and caverns.

Lake A considerable inland body of standing water.

Marsh A wetland fed by streams and with shallow or deep water. Often characterized by mats of cattail, bulrushes, sedges and wetland forbs.

Mesic A type of plant that requires a moderate amount of water.

Moraine Long, irregular hills of glacial till deposited by stagnant and retreating glaciers.

Natural Community A group of living organisms that live in the same place, e.g. woodland or prairie.

Park An area maintained in its natural state as a public property.

Pond A body of water usually smaller than a lake.

Prairie Primarily treeless grassland community characterized by full sun and dominated by perennial, native grasses and forbs. Isolated remnants of tall grass prairie can be found along and near the I&M Corridor.

Preserve An area restricted for the protection and preservation of natural resources.

Ridge A range of hills or mountains.

Savanna A grassland ecosystem with scattered trees characterized by native grasses and forbs.

Sedges Grass-like plants with triangular stems and without showy flowers. Many are dominant in sedge meadows, bogs and fens but others are found in woodlands or prairies.

Shrubs Low woody plants, usually shorter than trees and with several stems.

Swale A lower lying or depressed and off wet stretch of land.

Swamp Spongy land saturated and sometimes partially or intermittently covered with water.

Turf The upper stratum of soil bound by grass and plant roots into a thick mat.

Wetland The low lying wet area between higher ridges.

Riding Tips

- Pushing in gears that are too high can push knees beyond their limits. Avoid extremes by pedaling faster rather than shifting into a higher gear.

- Keeping your elbows bent, changing your hand position frequently and wearing bicycle gloves all help to reduce the numbness or pain in the palm of the hand from long-distance riding.

- Keep you pedal rpms up on an uphill so you have reserve power if you lose speed.

- Stay in a high-gear on a level surface, placing pressure on the pedals and resting on the handle bars and saddle.

- Lower your center of gravity on a long or steep downhill run by using the quick release seat post binder and dropping the saddle height down.

- Brake intermittently on a rough surface.

- Wear proper equipment. Wear a helmet that is approved by the Snell Memorial Foundation or the American National Standards Institute. Look for one of their stickers inside the helmet.

- Use a lower tire inflation pressure for riding on unpaved surfaces. The lower pressure will provide better tire traction and a more comfortable ride.

- Apply your brakes gradually to maintain control on loose gravel or soil.

- Ride only on trails designated for bicycles or in areas where you have the permission of the landowner.

- Be courteous to hikers or horseback riders on the trail, they have the right of way.

- Leave riding trails in the condition you found them. Be sensitive to the environment. Properly dispose of your trash. If you open a gate, close it behind you.

- Don't carry items or attach anything to your bicycle that might hinder your vision or control.

- Don't wear anything that restricts your hearing.

- Don't carry extra clothing where it can hang down and jam in a wheel.

Explanation of Symbols

SYMBOL LEGEND	
🏊	Beach/Swimming
🚲	Bicycle Repair
🏠	Cabin
⛺	Camping
🛶	Canoe Launch
➕	First Aid
🍴	Food
GC	Golf Course
❓	Information
🛏	Lodging
MF	Multi-Facilities
P	Parking
🧺	Picnic
🏛	Ranger Station
🚻	Restrooms
🏠	Shelter
T	Trailhead
🏛	Visitor/Nature Center
💧	Water
🔭	Overlook/Observation

TRAIL LEGEND	
▬▬▬▬	Bike/Multi Trail
●●●●●●●	Hiking only Trail
▬·▬·▬·▬	XC Skiing only
========	Planned Trail
▬ ▬ ▬ ▬	Alternate Trail
▬▬▬▬	Road/Highway
+++++++	Railroad Tracks

AREA LEGEND	
▢	City, Town
▢	Parks, Preserves
▢	Waterway
▢	Marsh/Wetland
▬▬	Mileage Scale
★	Points of Interest
– –	County/State
🌲	Forest/Woods

TRAIL USES LEGEND	
🚴	Leisure Biking
🚵	Mountain Biking
🚶	Hiking
⛷	Cross-country Skiing
🐎	Horseback Riding
🛼	Rollerblading
	Other

Indiana & Kentucky Sectionals

Northern Indiana

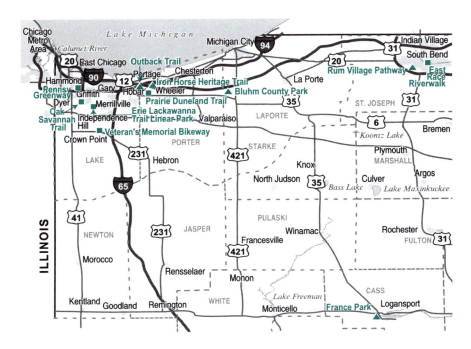

Trail Name	Page No.
Bluhm County Park	20
Bonneyville Mill County Park	22
East Race Riverwalk	24
France Park	26
J.B. Franke Park	28
Keklonga Trail	30
Lake City Greenway	32
Nickel Plate Trail	35

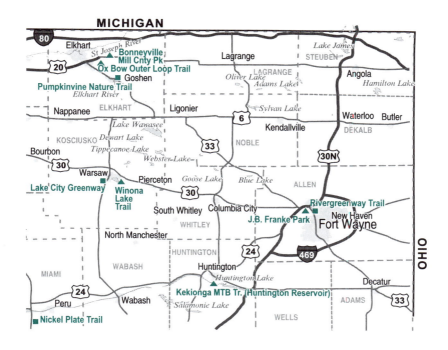

Trail Name	Page No.
Northwest Indiana Regional Bikeways	38
Veterans Memorial Trail	39
Pennsy Greenway	39
Ironhorse Heritage Trail	39
Erie Lackawana Trail	40
Oak Savannah Trail	42
Prairie Duneland Trail	44
Calumet Trail	46
Outback Trail	48
Ox Bow County Park	50
Pumpkinvine Nature Trail	52
Rivergreenway	54
Rum Village Annex	58
Winona Lake Trail	60

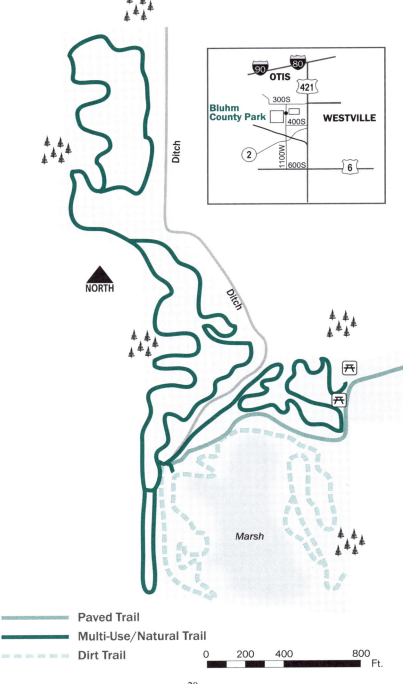

Bluhm County Park

Trail Uses

Vicinity   Westville

Trail Length 5 miles

Surface   Singletrack

County   LaPorte

Trail Notes   The setting for this 96 acre park consists of upland forest, wetland, prairie, a stocked pond and spring wildflowers. There are frequent, steep but short hills with many tight turns and intersections, plus tree roots thrown in for good measure. Effort level is moderate. In addition to biking, the trail is open to hikers, cross-country skiers and equestrians. The trail can get muddy following rainy weather.

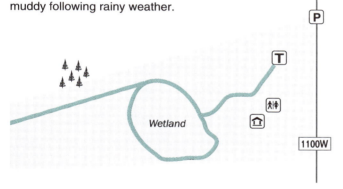

Getting There   Take Hwy 421 south from I-94 or the Toll Road to County Road 300 South. Take CR 300 west to County Road 1100 West, then south for about a mile to Bluhm County Park on the right side. Follow the easement for about a quarter mile to the trailhead in West Woods.

Contact   Bluhm County Parks Dept.   219-325-8315

Bonneyville Mill County Park

Trail Uses

Vicinity Bristol

Trail Length 7 miles

Surface Wood chip

County Elkhart

Trail Notes This 223 acre park features rolling hills, woodlands, marshes, and open meadows. The 7 miles of nature and biking trails meander around and through the park providing frequent opportunities to view the beautiful wildflowers and abundant wildlife. There are five shelters and numerous picnic tables. Each shelter provides water, restrooms, and picnic table facilities. Shelters need to be reserved. The fire tower at the extreme end of the South Farm is a focal point and destination. The trail crosses County Road 8 at well-marked points to connect within the northern Mill Area. The park opens at 8 am and closes at 7 pm, except for November, December & January when it closes at 6 pm. There is no entrance fee.

Getting There Bonneyville Mill County Park is located 2.5 miles southeast of Bristol at 53373 County Road 131, south of State Road 120.

Contact Elkhart County Park & Recreation Dept.
574-535-6458

SYMBOL LEGEND

- Beach/Swimming
- Bicycle Repair
- Cabin
- Camping
- Canoe Launch
- First Aid
- Food
- Golf Course
- Information
- Lodging
- Multi-Facilities
- Parking
- Picnic
- Ranger Station
- Restrooms
- Shelter
- Trailhead
- Visitor/Nature Center
- Water
- Overlook/Observation

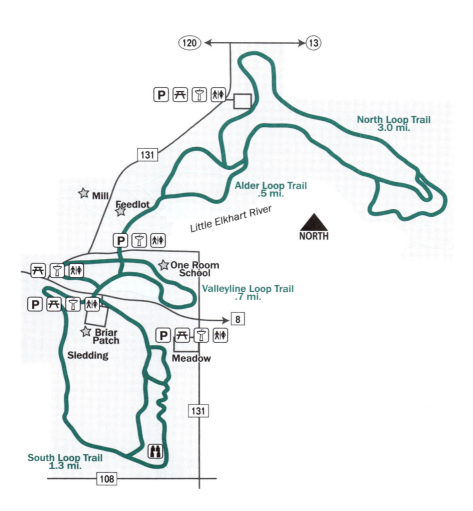

East Race Riverwalk

Trail Uses

Vicinity South Bend

Trail Length 9 miles

Surface Concrete

County St. Joseph

Trail Notes The East Race Riverwalk, a riverbank greenbelt pathway, is located along the St. Joseph River in South Bend. It stretches from Veteran's Memorial Park up along the East Race Waterway, around Madison Center to the north, then back down the west side of the river past Bicentennial Park to Karl King Tower. The setting varies from intimate quiet stretches to dramatic white water scenes. There are abundant way stops along the path, including three major parks, restaurants, gift, and specialty shops.

Getting There Veteran's Memorial Park is located off Hildreth Avenue just north of the St. Joseph River and east of Hwy 31. Madison Center is located just north of the intersection of Madison and Niles Streets.

Contact South Bend Parks & Recreation 574-235-9414

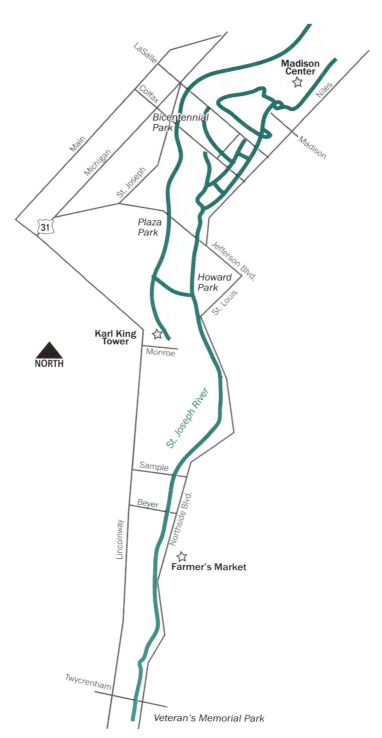

France Park

Trail Uses	
Vicinity	Logansport, Monticello
Trail Length	10 miles
Surface	Singletrack, fire roads
County	Cass

Trail Notes This multiple-use trail system winds through woods, prairies, quarries and creeks. Effort level in this 515 acre park varies from moderate to difficult, with many hills and switchbacks, plus fast and rocky areas. There is a riding fee. Park features include a swimming lake, rentable shelters, and camping facilities, both primitive and modern. The swimming lake is an abandoned spring-fed quarry popular with scuba divers. The modern camping facilities offer bathrooms, showers, water, and electrical hook-ups.

Trailheads

Trailhead #1 Begins at the rocky trail surrounding the Old Kenith Stone Quarry. Expect a challenging ride with scenic views.

Trailhead #2 Begins at the main parking lot and follows the towpath of the old Wabash-Erie Canal.

Trailhead #3 Begins at the boat ramp and follows the Paw Paw Creek.

Trailhead #4 Begins just above the waterfall of the Paw Paw Creek and takes you to an overlook site.

Trailhead #5 Begins at the Wabash River Picnic Area and winds up through the Whispering Pine Path.

Getting There From Logansport, take Hwy 24 west for about a half mile. Turn left (south) into France Park and follow the road into the parking area.

Contact France Park   574-753-2928

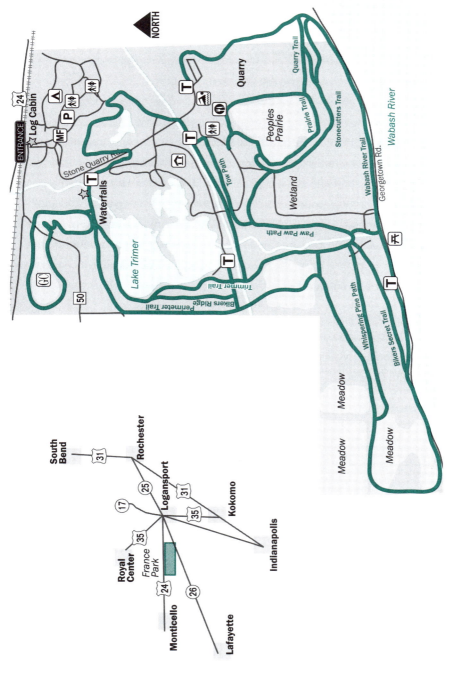

J.B. Franke Park

Trail Uses

Vicinity Fort Wayne

Trail Length 10 miles

Surface Singletrack

County Allen

Trail Notes This 280 acre park provides a variety of trails through rolling woodlands. You will experience challenging twists and turns, combined with some both short and some steep climbs. The trails are predominantly singletrack with many loops. One of the trails takes you along a cliff and another along a streambed. Effort level is moderate. There are two racecourses at the back of the park. The BMX track will test your skills with its camelback hills and sharp turns. From the top of the soapbox derby track you will have a scenic view of the park and its surrounds.

Getting There From the north side of Fort Wayne take I-69, Exit 109A, and proceed southeasterly on Gosher Avenue to Sherman Blvd. Take a left on Sherman for 0.4 miles into Franke Park's main entrance, and follow the road to the Nature Center.

Contact Fort Wayne Parks Dept. 260-427-6000

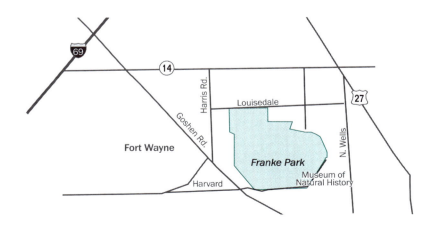

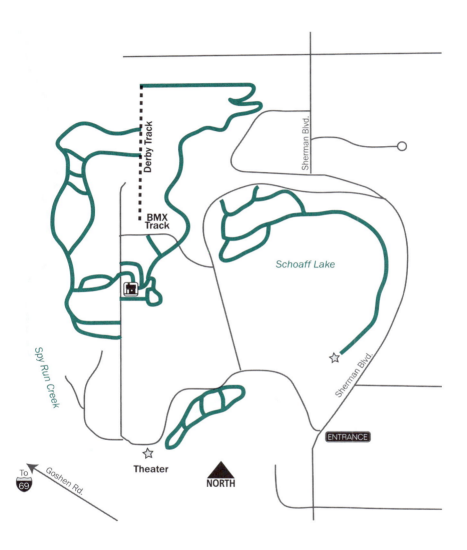

Kekionga Trail– Huntington Lake Recreation Area

Trail Uses

Vicinity Huntington

Trail Length 12 miles

Surface Doubletrack, singletrack

County Huntington

Trail Notes Huntington Reservoir, renamed Roush Lake in honor of former US Congressman J. Edward Roush, was opened in 1970 as a flood-control reservoir. The trail is mostly rolling terrain, doubletrack and very fast. There are a few decent climbs, and two technical ravines. When water levels are high, some of this dirt trail can be under water. After the water recedes, washouts are common. The trail is cleared several times a year by park employees. The 870 acre lake is surrounded by this 7,400 acre property.

Getting There From Fort Wayne, take I-69 south for about 7 miles to US 24 (Exit 102). Take US 24 west for almost 19 miles to Hwy 5. Go south on Hwy 5 for about 2 miles to downtown Huntington. Proceed south on Hwy 224/Hwy 5 for 2.1 miles to Little Turtle State Recreation Area. Signs will take you to the Mountain Bike Trailhead.

Contact Huntington State Recreation Area   260-468-2165

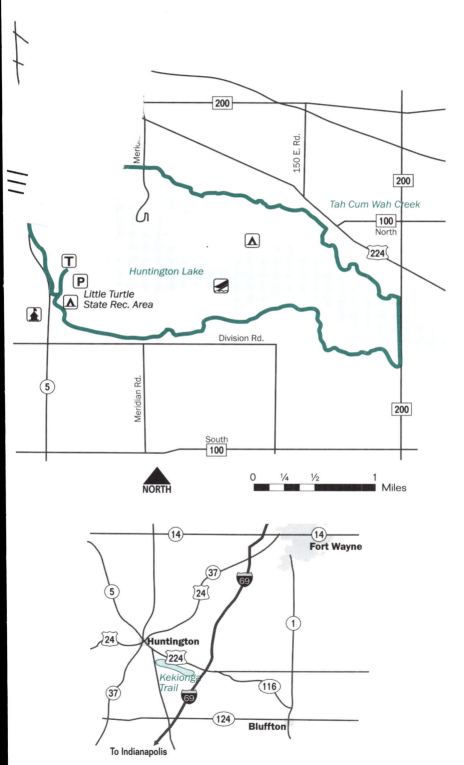

Lake City Greenway

Trail Uses

Vicinity   Warsaw, Winona Lake

Trail Length   8 miles (including pending or planned)

Surface   Asphalt, boardwalk

County   Kosciusko

Trail Notes   About 4.7 miles are open or in the works. The trail will be between 8 and 10 foot wide. It will run from the Chinworth Bridge on Old Road 30 west of Warsaw, connecting with Central Park and the Central Business District in Warsaw, ending by Winona Lake Town Park. The Beyer Farm Trail consists of a long boardwalk across the wetlands on the south shore of Pike Lake, with an asphalt section at each end. In addition, there is a 2 mile path to the City-County Athletic Complex and Chinworth Bridge on the west side, and another 2 mile section through the town of Winona Lake. The project includes a combination of existing public right-or-ways, a portion of a railroad corridor, a utility easement, a county drainage ditch, and some private property.

Getting There   Warsaw is located at the intersection of Hwy's 15 and 110, less than two miles south of Hwy 30. From Main Street, follow Cook Street north to Arthur Street and Park. Turn right. The trail follows the path between the cemetery and the lake.

Contact   City of Warsaw Community Development Coordinator
                     574-372-9549

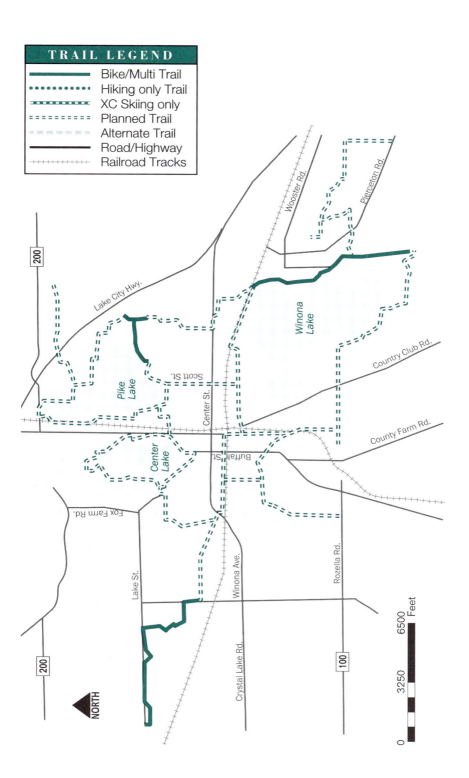

Nickel Plate Trail

Trail Uses	
Vicinity	Rochester, Kokomo
Trail Length	15 miles (over 40 miles when complete)
Surface	Asphalt, crushed stone, dirt, grass
County	Miami, Fulton, Howard

Trail Notes The trail is being developed along a section of the former New York, Chicago & St. Louis RR, nicknamed the Nickel Plate. Generally, the Nickel Plate Trail is relatively flat and well tended, with a mix of open and tree-canopied areas. Along the east side of the corridor south of Bunker Hill, you can still see remnants of the electric interurban rail line, abandoned around 1940. The setting is typical of rural north central Indiana with woodlands, wetlands and an abundance of plant and animal species.

Fifteen miles of trail are currently open in three separate sections. South of Peru 3.4 miles of the trail are paved. This scenic section follows the Little Pike Creek. Just south of the trailhead is an interesting old dam. There is an open rustic section running 2.5 miles from Bennetts Switch north to 1050S in Miami and one mile south to CR1360S, which is south of SR18. Caution is suggested if you use the trail on the north side of Miami because of problems with neighborhood dogs. Under development is an asphalt trail all the way to Bunker Hill, and a section heading north and connecting to the existing Riverwalk. Plans call for the trail to eventually connect Kokomo, Peru and Rochester, and become part of the American Discovery Trail.

Getting There The trail corridor is located just east of US31. Follow US31 south of Plymouth or north of Kokomo to get to Miami County.

Contact Nickel Plate Trail, Inc.
PO Box 875
Peru, Indiana 46970
email: webmaster@nickelplatetrail.org

Nickel Plate Trail (continued)

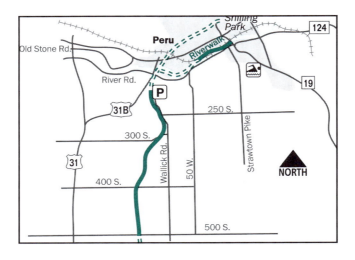

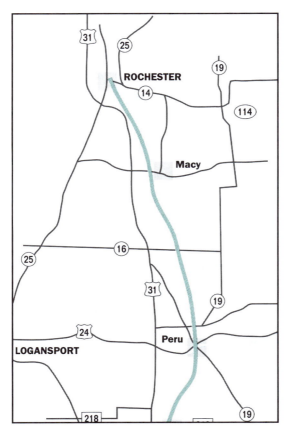

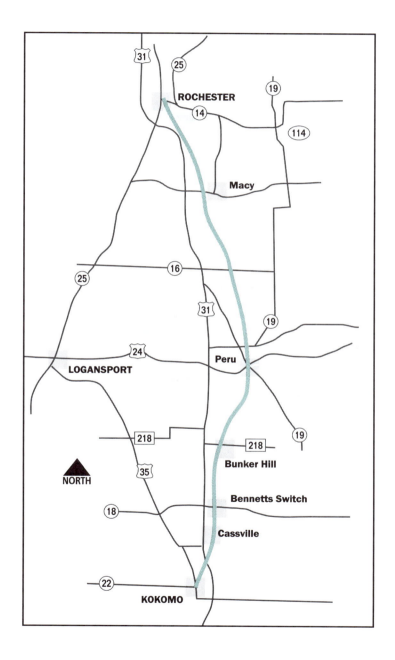

Northwest Indiana Regional Bikeways

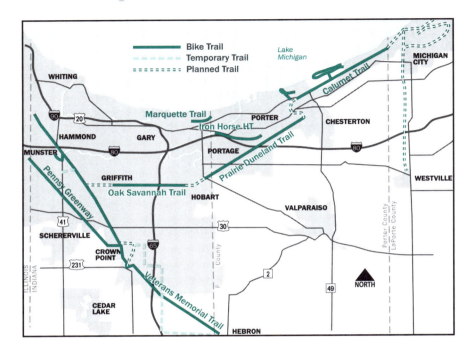

Pennsy Greenway

Crown Point to Lansing, Illinois

This planned trail will cover 10 miles in Indiana and 5 miles in Illinois. It will transverse the communities of Crown Point, Schererville, Munster, Dyer, Lansing, Calumet City and Burnham. Ground breaking has begun on the Illinois side, and will be the first off-road, bi-state link in the region.

Iron Horse Heritage Trail

This 5.1 mile trail is located between the Porter/Lake County line and the Prairie Duneland Trail. It spans the city of Portage. The surface is sand, dirt, and partially paved. A unique feature planned is dual surfacing, providing a hard asphalt surface, plus a limestone surface for joggers.

Northwest Indiana Regional Bikeways
Veterans Memorial Trail

Trail Uses

Vicinity   Crown Point

Trail Length   9 miles

Surface   Under development

County   Lake

Trail Notes   Construction of this planned trail is expected to be completed in 2008 or 2009. The trail will follow the abandoned Pennsylvania Railroad along US231 and will connect with the Pennsy Greenway project at Crown Point, which in turn will go to the Illinois state line. This is the first trail in the United States named in honor of our veterans. Seven of these planned 9 miles will have an equestrian trail paralleling the bike/hike path.

Contact   Lake County Parks & Recreation Dept. 219-945-0543

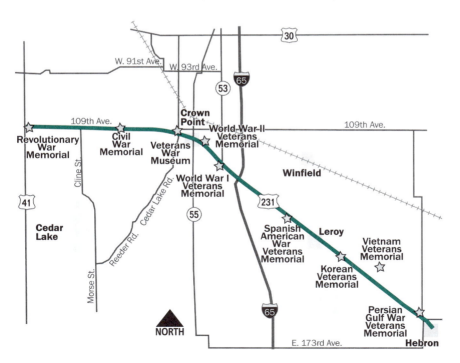

Northwest Indiana Regional Bikeways

Erie Lackawanna Trail

Trail Uses

Vicinity Crown Point, Highland

Trail Length 14 miles (11.25 miles with the not yet connected Hammond section)

Surface Asphalt

County Lake

Trail Notes The southern portion of the trail is built along a wide, grassy right-of-way and passes through fields, wetlands and neighborhoods. The designers took advantage of the extra space to give the asphalt a tight, wavy pattern, instead of the typically straight rail-trail. Gazebos, benches, and painted brick surfacing invite your unplanned stops. As your ride takes you toward Griffith and Highland, the trail becomes suburban and urban, passing several schools, the old town centers, and across active multi-lane streets and active railroads. The trail currently ends to the north in Highland near I-94, among a string of electric towers.

The trail will eventually connect to the Hammond section upon completion of the trail along the Little Calumet River. Highland's section is called the Crosstown Trail. Plans also include connecting the trail southward through Crown Point to the Veterans Memorial Trail. Longer range plans might also bring cyclists by trail into Chicago.

Getting There From Crown Point/Merrillville, take SR55 to 93rd Street, then turn to the west. Trailhead & parking are on the right about a 1/3 mile further.

Contact Highland Parks & Recreation Dept.   219-838-0114

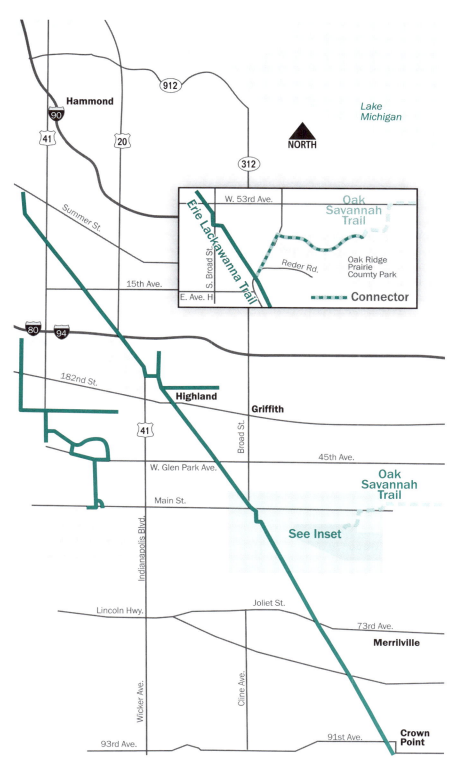

Northwest Indiana Regional Bikeways
Oak Savannah Trail

Trail Uses	🚲 🚶 ⛸
Vicinity	Hobart, Griffith
Trail Length	7.5 miles
Surface	Asphalt
Counties	Lake, Porter

Trail Notes   This nearly straight trail currently runs from Oak Ridge Prairie County Park in Griffith eastward through Gary to Hobart ending at Wisconsin Street. There are pit toilets and picnic area facilities at the Oak Ridge Prairie County Park. The ride takes you through savannahs, remnant prairies, wetlands, lakes, parks, and residential neighborhoods. The trail will eventually run through Hobart to link with the Prairie-Duneland Trail. There are several at-grade road crossings, so use caution. Because of heavy traffic at the Broadway intersection, it is recommended you travel one block south via sidewalks and cross at the 53rd Avenue stoplight.

An oak savannah ecosystem is a transition area between tallgrass prairie and oak woodland, which received enough sunlight and shade for both ecosystems to thrive. Oak savannah was once common in northern Indiana, but has been encroached by development.

Getting There   East Trailhead – Wisconsin Street in Hobart. Following the Hobart break, the eastern segment may be assessed from a gravel parking lot at the northeast corner of Cleveland Street and SR 51 in Hobart. West Trailhead – Oak Ridge Prairie Park in Griffith.

Contact   Lake County Parks & Recreation   219-945-0543

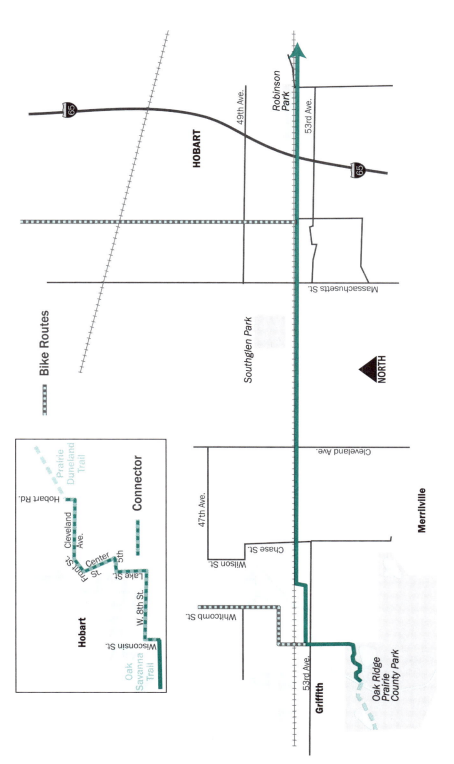

Northwest Indiana Regional Bikeways
Prairie Duneland Trail

Trail Uses

Vicinity Porter, Chesterton

Trail Length 10 miles

Surface Asphalt

County Portage, Lake

Trail Notes The Prairie Duneland Trail traverses some of most scenic natural area in the state. The abundant species of flora and fauna found along this unique ecosystem gave the trail its name. Restrooms are available in Olsen Park, midway through the ride. There is a planned trail extension southwestward through Hobart to connect with the Old Savannah Trail. Also planned is the 3.5 mile Port Brickyard Trail that will connect the east end of the Prairie Duneland Trail to the Calumet Trail to the north.

Getting There Take I-94 to Portage at Willowcreek Road and drive south. Continue past the curves to the Prairie Duneland trailhead at the tunnel. There are also trailheads at SR51 in Hobart, on Swanson Road, and at the Chesterton terminus.

Contact Portage Park Dept. 219-762-1675

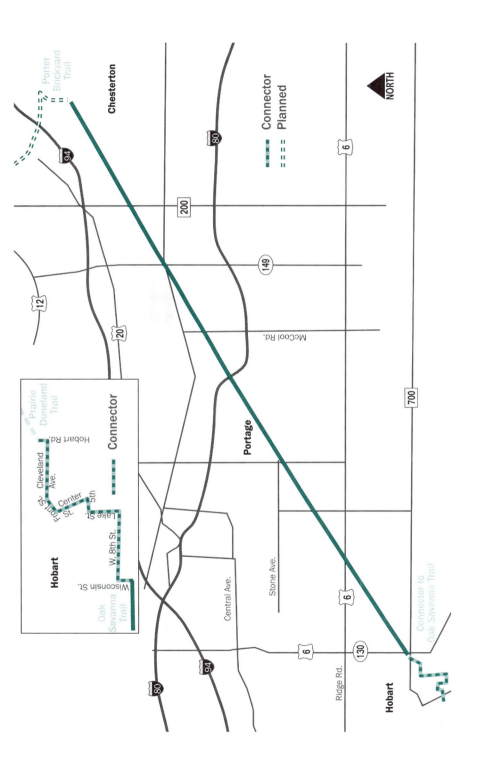

Northwest Indiana Regional Bikeways

Calumet Trail

Trail Uses	
Vicinity	Michigan City, Chesterton
Trail Length	9 miles
Surface	Crushed Limestone
County	Porter

Trail Notes   The Calumet Trail parallels US 12 just to the north, and skirts the south side of the Indiana Dunes State Park. It was built on a Northern Indiana Public Service Co. right of way and runs parallel with the South Shore railroad tracks. There are restroom facilities at the west end, but no water on the trail. The western terminus is on Mineral Springs Road near Cowles Bog. You can extend your ride by another six miles by detouring north a half mile. The planned 3.5 mile Porter Brickyard Trail will provide a connection to the Prairie Duneland Trail.

Getting There   From Michigan City take Hwy 12 west for about 12 miles to Dune Acres Road. Turn right on Dune Acres Road and go 0.2 miles to the parking area on the left.

Contact   Porter County Parks Dept.   219-465-3586

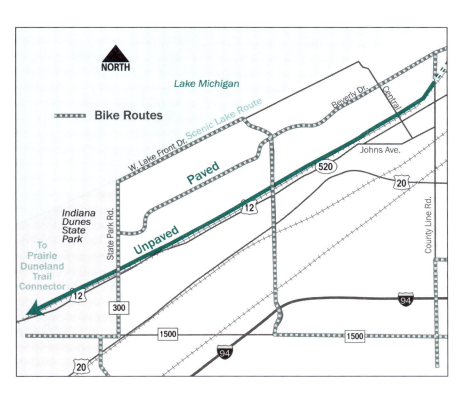

The Indian Dunes

Outback Trail

Trail Uses	
Vicinity	Portage
Trail Length	11 miles
Surface	Singletrack
County	Porter

Trail Notes The Outback Trail is located at Imagination Glen Park in Portage. There are over 11 miles of scenic groomed trails available for mountain biking and hiking. The setting is woods with a couple of steep hills. Effort level varies from easy to difficult. The trail should not be ridden when wet as it then becomes slick and spotted with mud holes. The trail is popular with both locals and out-of-towners, and is available for races and other events.

Getting There From Central Avenue and Willowcreek Road in downtown Portage, take Central Avenue to its end at McCool Road. Proceed left (north) to the entrance for Imagination Glen Park just before the road starts to curve. Take a right inside the park to the trailhead parking where the trail begins at the Kiosk sign.

Contact Portage Director of Sports   219-762-1675

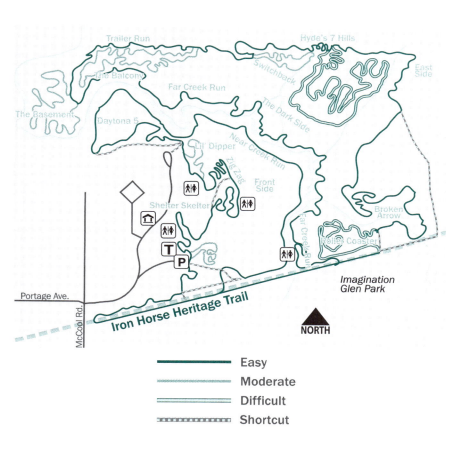

Ox Bow County Park

Trail Uses	
Vicinity	Goshen
Trail Length	8 miles
Surface	5 miles wood chip, 1 mile paved, 2 miles groomed outer loop
County	Elkhart

Trail Notes This nature trail leads you through meadows, marshes, woodlands and prairies. Wildlife is common, and includes deer, fox, and raccoons. Shelters are scattered throughout the park, and each has drinking fountains, primitive restrooms, and outdoor grills. Additional park facilities include picnic areas, an observation tower, athletic fields, and a canoe launch. The park opens at 8 am and closes between 6 pm and 9 pm depending on the season. There is a vehicle entrance fee during posted hours.

Getting There Ox Bow County Park is located on County Road 45, north of US Hwy 33, midway between Elkhart and Goshen.

Contact Elkhart County Park & Recreation Dept.
574-535-6458

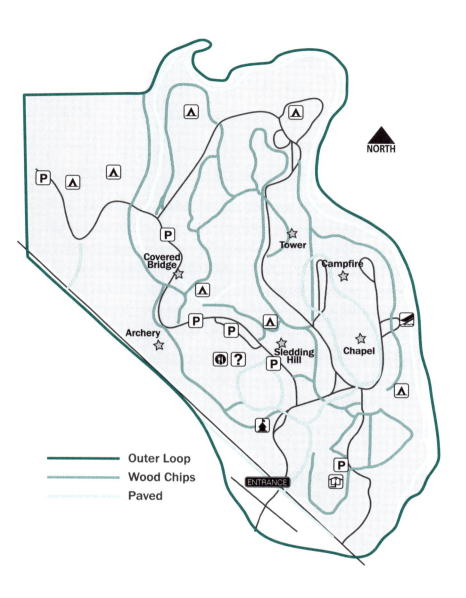

Pumpkinvine Nature Trail

Trail Uses

Vicinity Goshen, Middlebury, Shipshewana

Trail Length 17 miles (partially completed)

Surface Asphalt, crushed limestone

Counties Elkhart, LaGrange

Trail Notes This is a linear park and greenway trail under construction, mostly on the former "Pumpkinvine" railroad corridor. A large portion of the Pumpkinvine Trail is canopied with trees creating a tranquil corridor. The trail passes through agricultural countryside and several communities. There are six wooden pile bridges, including the 160 foot bridge across the Little Elkhart River near Kinder Park. Three tunnels are proposed: under US 20, County Roads 22 and 37.

Getting There Current accesses include: Kinder Park, located at the intersection of Bristol and Pleasant in Middlebury; and Abshire Park, located off Hwy 4, east of Hwy 15 in Goshen.

Contact Friends of the Pumpkinvine Nature Trail
PO Box 392
Goshen, IN 46527
www.pumpkinvine.org

Trail Development Schedule

Phase	Miles	Access	Status
1	1.75	Abshire Park, Goshen	Open
2	0.65	Krider Park, Middlebury	Open
3	2.40	Rider Park	2008*
4	5.30	Wolfe Park, Shipshewana	2008*
5A	3.10	Abshire Park	2012*
5B	1.70	On country roads	
5C	1.55	Krider Park	2011*
6	1.20	Krider Park	2015*

*planned construction

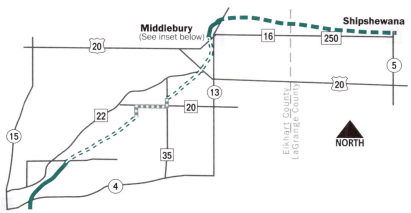
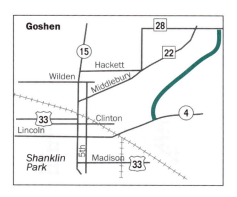

Rivergreenway

Trail Uses

Vicinity Fort Wayne

Trail Length 25 miles total (100 miles planned)

Pathways	Trail Length
St. Mary's River Pathway	8.75 miles
Maumee River Pathway	8.75 miles
St. Joseph River Pathway	3.00 m.iles
St. Joe Boulevard Pathway	1.14 miles
Circle of Hope	2.00 miles
Jefferson Trail	1.11 miles

Surface Concrete, asphalt, boardwalks

County Allen

Trail Notes

St. Marys River

The pathway begins at the confluence of the three rivers and runs west and south to Tillman Park. Future plans include a link to the St. Mary's River Pathway from Lawton Park to Franke Park, and from Swinney Park to the University of St. Francis. Each mile is identified by 12 inch granite markers. The major accesses are the Three Rivers Trailhead, Lawton Park, Bloomingdale Park, Swinney Park, Foster Park, Fairfield Avenue Trailhead, and Tillman Park. Parking is available at all the parks along the route.

Maumee River Pathway

This pathway also begins at the confluence of the three rivers, and runs west to Spy Run Avenue, then south to Main Street. From the south side of Main Street, the path runs east to Clay Street, crosses Clay, and then heads north and northeast across the Columbia Street Bridge. After crossing the bridge, the path heads east following the Maumee River. It ends at Moser Park in New Haven. Plans call for the pathway to be extended with New Haven's greenways and the Maumee River Heritage Trail. Major accesses are the Three Rivers Trailhead, North River Road Trailhead, and Kreager Park. Each mile is identified by 12 inch granite markers.

St. Joe River Pathway

Beginning at the confluence of the three rivers the pathway ends at Johnny Appleseed Park just south of Coliseum Boulevard. The trail will eventually be extended to Shoaff Park. Major accesses are the Three Rivers Trailhead and the Johnny Appleseed Park Trailhead. Each mile is identified by 12 inch granite markers.

St. Joe Boulevard Pathway

This pathway runs on the east side of the St. Joseph River from State Blvd. to Lafayette Street. The surface is concrete, and the major access is the Three River Trailhead.

Downtown Rotary Club Circle of Hope

Located in Fort Wayne's downtown area. Major accesses are at Headwaters Park, Three Rivers Trailhead, and Lawton Park.

West Jefferson Trail

The pathway begins at West Swinney Park at the St. Mary's River Pathway, and runs west through the park and then along West Jefferson Blvd. to Rockhill Park. It will eventually be extended as the 3.5 mile Towpath Trail.

Contact Fort Wayne Greenways Manager   260-427-6002

Rivergreenway (continued)

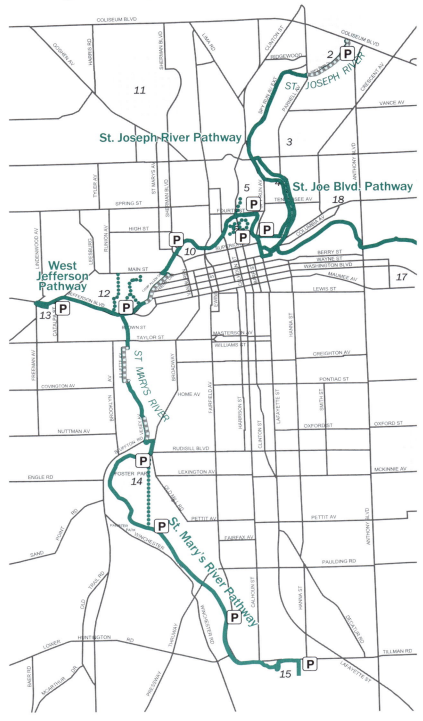

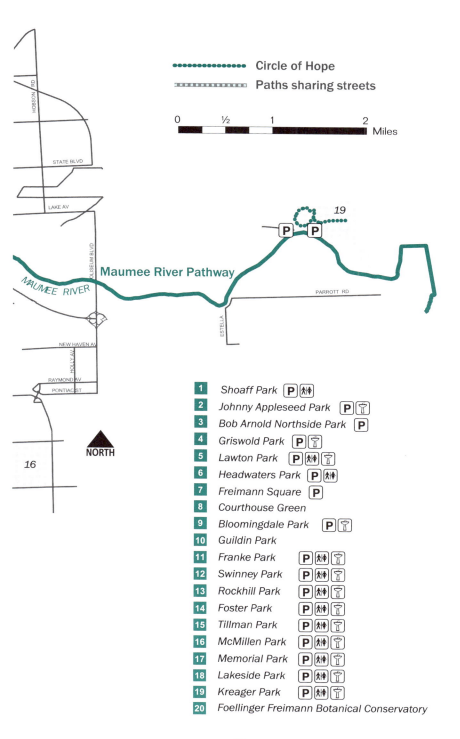

Rum Village Annex

Trail Uses	
Vicinity	South Bend
Trail Length	6 miles
Surface	Singletrack
County	St. Joseph

Trail Notes A lot of trail is crammed into this small park area. There are trail sections for all levels, from beginners to advanced cyclists. The trails to the far right lead to the easy-to-moderate section. The middle leads to the more moderate-to-difficult section. The trail system is one way, with blue arrows displayed throughout the course to remind you. The Rum Village Annex is located just outside the west gate to the main Rum Village Park in South Bend's southwest side. There are some quick climbs and descents, and tight turns. Tree roots and fallen trees serve as frequent obstacles. The setting is mostly flat woods. The trail system was developed and is maintained by the Northern Indiana Mountain Biking Association.

Getting There From US 20 on the south side of South Bend, take Hwy 31 North into South Bend. Turn left onto Chippewa Avenue, then right onto Gertrude for about a half mile to the trailhead on the right. You can park across the street from the trailhead or in the park, a little further north on Gertrude Street.

Contact South Bend Park & Recreation 219-272-4864

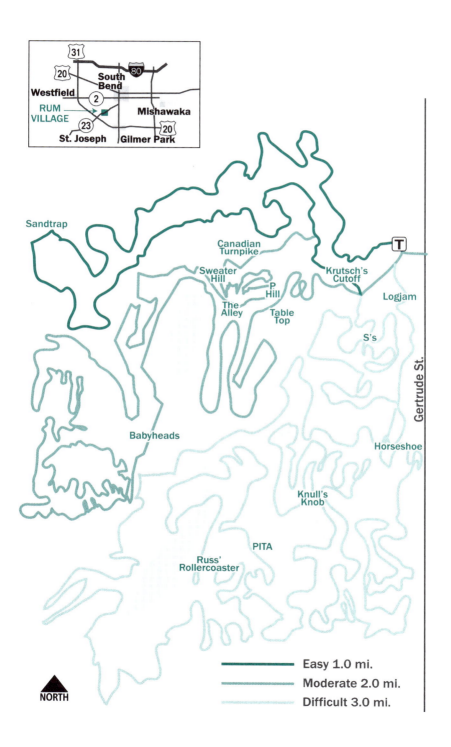

Winona Lake Trail

Trail Uses	🚵
Vicinity	Warsaw
Trail Length	10 miles
Surface	Singletrack
County	Kosciusko

Trail Notes This trail system offers a variety of diverse terrain, from flat and smooth to tight turns and short, steep climbs. There are a lot of elevation changes. Effort level varies from easy to difficult. There is a water crossing, a ramp over a small ravine on the east side of the creek, and a suspended bridge. Expect frequent run-ins with logs, rocks, stumps and roots. You should ride clockwise if you take the loop trail on the east side of the creek.

Getting There From Hwy 30 in Warsaw, take Center Street west to Argonne Road. Proceed south (left) on Argonne Road until it ends at Winona Road. Past the light on Winona Road, then Park Avenue south (it runs alongside the lake) to Boys City Drive. Turn left on Boys City Drive, crossing a bridge at a creek to its end, which is the entrance. Park at the Winona Lake Park parking lot. The trailhead is about a $1/4$ mile further.

Contact Village of Winona   574-268-9888

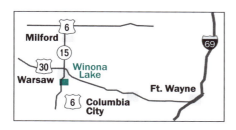

Central Indiana

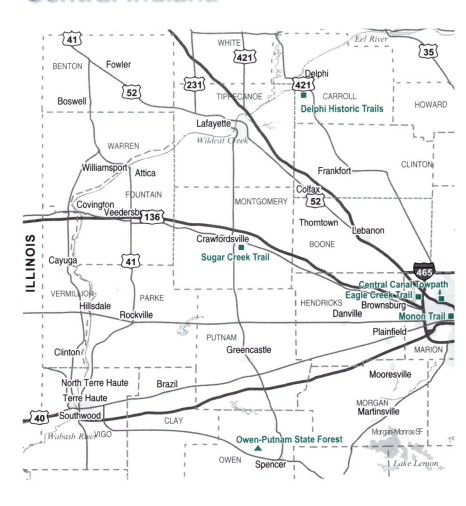

Trail Name	Page No.
Cardinal Greenway	66
Central Canal Towpath	68
Delphi Historic Trails	70
Eagle Creek Trail	72
Fall Creek Trail	74
Monon Trail & Monon Greenway	76

Trail Name	Page No.
Owen-Putnam State Forest	80
Pleasant Run Trail	82
Pogue's Run Trail	84
Sugar Creek Community Trail	86
Town Run Trail Park	88
Westwood Park	90
White River Wapahani Trail	92

Indianapolis Greenways

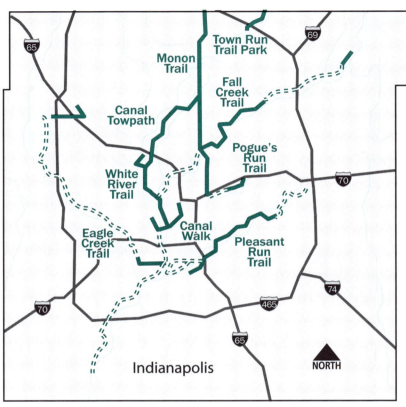

Courtesy of the Indianapolis Parks and Recreation Department

Courtesy of the Indianapolis Parks and Recreation Department

Cardinal Greenway

Trail Uses	🚵 🚶 ⛷ 🧲 🛼
Vicinity	Muncie, Medford, Gaston
Trail Length	20 miles
Surface	Asphalt
County	Delaware

Trail Notes This asphalt paved trail will eventually connect northward to Marion & Sweetser, and southward to Richmond, bringing the total length to almost 75 miles. The trail is mostly level with only some very slight inclines. About a third of the trail runs along US 35 so it is noisy and open, and can be gusty. The southern trailhead begins in farm fields, which are secluded and quiet until you hit the portion that is next to the highway. After Medford, the trail meets US 35. From the northern trailhead you'll pass many backyards with city streets to cross, although most are not heavily traveled. Horseback riding is permitted south from the Medford trailhead.

Attractions along the route include:
Wysor Street Depot – houses the Delaware Greenways office, several exhibits, a gift shop and historic memorabilia.
Prairie Creek Lake – located ¾ mile from the south trailhead in Delaware County. This large lake offers sailing, boating, windsailing, nearby walking trails, a model aircraft field, and a campground with modern facilities.

Getting There Southern trailhead in Mt. Pleasant – take US 35 to Mt. Pleasant. Just after passing through Mt. Pleasant look for CR 532E on your left. There is also a directional sign to Prairie Creek Reservoir at this intersection. Turn north for about 300 feet to the trailhead on your left (west).

Medford trailhead – located 3.1 miles north of CR542 on CR600S at Medford. The equestrian trail begins here and goes south to Prairie Creek. The earthen horse trail is on the west side of the Cardinal Greenway.

Northern trailhead – The Cardinal Greenway Deport parking lot in downtown Muncie serves as the northern trailhead. Take I-69 to the SR332 Exit. Go east on SR332 for about 9 miles into Muncie. This state road becomes McGalliard Road in Muncie. Continue to Wheeling Avenue, and turn right (south). Continue south for about a mile, where you cross the High Street Bridge. Immediately turn left (east) onto Wysor Street past Madison (3 traffic lights). The Cardinal Greenway Depot parking lot is 2 blocks east of Madison Street on the left.

Contact   Cardinal Greenways 765-287-0399

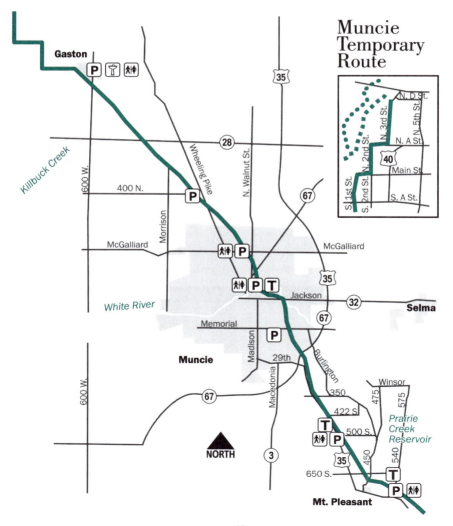

Central Canal Towpath

Trail Uses	
Vicinity	Indianapolis
Trail Length	5.2 miles
Surface	Crushed limestone, paved
County	Marion

Trail Notes The Central Canal Towpath travels from Broad Ripple to its south trailhead at 30th Street, passing many tourist sites. It connects to the Monon Trail, the White River Wapahani Trail, and a cross-downtown connection composed of St. Clair and Dorman Streets, making it a lynchpin of the Greenways loop. The surface is crushed limestone with a paved section from Guilford Avenue to the Monon Trail in Broad Ripple Village. The effort level is easy and the terrain is flat.

Getting There From downtown Indianapolis, take I-65 to 30th Street. Go west on 30th Street for about 1.5 miles to White River Drive East, then north to Heslar Naval Armory. Park along the side of the road.

Contact Indianapolis Parks and Recreation 317-327-7431

SYMBOL LEGEND

Beach/Swimming	Multi-Facilities
Bicycle Repair	Parking
Cabin	Picnic
Camping	Ranger Station
Canoe Launch	Restrooms
First Aid	Shelter
Food	Trailhead
Golf Course	Visitor/Nature Center
Information	Water
Lodging	Overlook/Observation

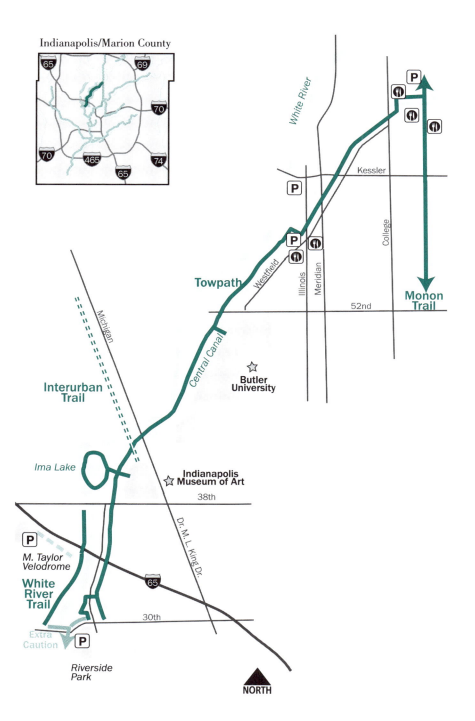

Delphi Historic Trails

Trail Uses	
Vicinity	Delphi
Trail Length	10 miles
Surface	Crushed limestone, dirt
County	Carroll

Trail Notes   Located in Delphi, in north central Indiana, the trails are mostly crushed limestone, packed, and wide. A few follow streets to connect parks. The ride includes historic bridges, a preserved section of the Wabash & Erie Canal and the new Canal Interpretive Center. The system includes 3 rail-trails, one of which is along the former Monon line between SR25 and Deer Creek.

There are three National Register Sites nearby – the Canal Construction Camp site; Lock #33 and adjacent lockkeeper's home site; and the 1857 Harley and Hubbard Lime Kiln site. There are also several interesting trails and loops in the southern system that radiate out from Trailhead Park alongside I-25. The northern half of this 2.5 mile section of the Canal appears like it did in the heyday of 1850's. The newest trail is called the Monon High Bridge Trail. It goes east of Delphi two miles from City Park and then follows a section of the old Monon line.

Getting There   You can take I-65 to Lafayette, then SR25 east, or take US35 to Logansport, and then west on SR25 to Delphi. At the Courthouse turn northwest and go about 6 clocks. Turn left and park at the Canal Interpretive Center. A convenient access point is located at Trailhead Park along Deer Creek one mile southwest of Delphi on I-25. Another point of access is Canal Park, 11 blocks north of the Court House stoplight on Washington Street.

Contact   Canal Hotline   765-564-6572

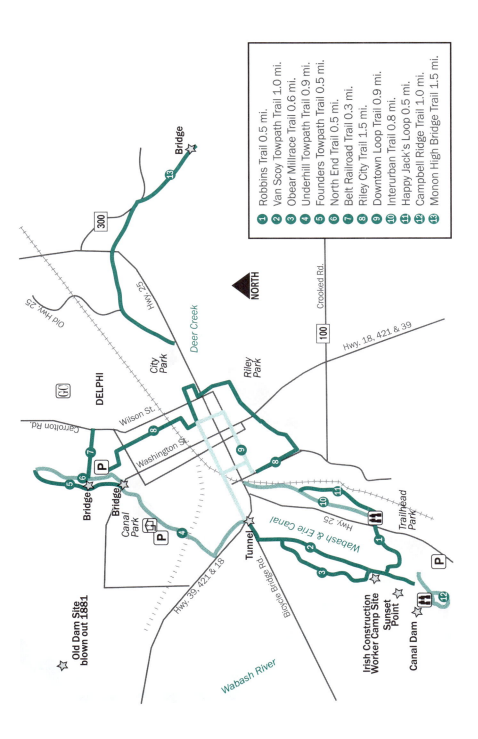

Eagle Creek Trail

Trail Uses

Vicinity   Indianapolis

Trail Length   3.8 miles complete with another 12 miles planned

Surface   Asphalt

County   Marion

Trail Notes   Currently 2 miles south at Raymond Street, and another 1.8 miles on the north end at 46th Street are complete. These sections are 8 to 12 feet wide and asphalt paved. Major access point will be Thatcher Park, Ridenour Park and Ross-Claypool Park. The south section connects with the White River Wapahani Trail. To the north the trail meanders past play fields at the Pike Youth Soccer Complex and the Mayor's Community Gardens. Secondary trails loop through woodland, prairie and wetland settings throughout the park.

Getting There   From Hwy 465 at Hwy 74, go northeast on Hwy 465 to 56th Street, then northwest to Eagle Creek Park where you will find parking and restrooms.

Contact   Indianapolis Parks & Recreation   317-327-7431

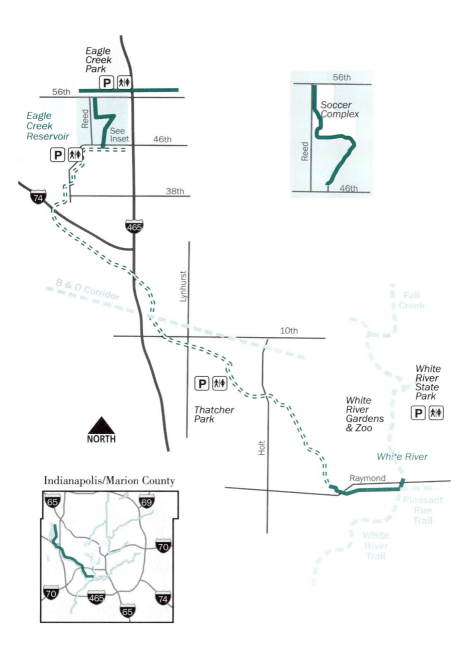

Fall Creek Trail

Trail Uses	
Vicinity	Indianapolis
Trail Length	7.2 miles
Surface	Asphalt
County	Marion

Trail Notes This is a wide, forested corridor, often brushing against Fall Creek along much of its way to its junction with the Monon Trail. The trail continues under the Keystone Avenue Bridge along Fall Creek to 38th Street, where a pedestrian activated signal is installed. The trail extends north to Skiles Test Park.

The Upper Fall Creek Loop Trail is a 1.5 mile separate section along Fall Creek Road, just south of 79th Street. It is surfaced with asphalt and loops a long, narrow overflow pond for Fall Creek. There is a parking lot adjacent to Fall Creek Road just south of 79th Street. There are plans to extend the Fall Creek Trail further north, making the Loop Trail a northern terminus.

Downstream, a short section of the trail connects to the White River Wapahani Trail where the Fall Creek flows into White River. The Dr. Beurt SerVass suspension bridge crosses Fall Creek to allow access to and from the IUPUI campus and White River State Park.

Getting There There are several parking areas and access points, such as the 4400 block of Fall Creek Parkway, east of Keystone Avenue.

Contact Indianapolis Parks & Recreation 317-327-7431

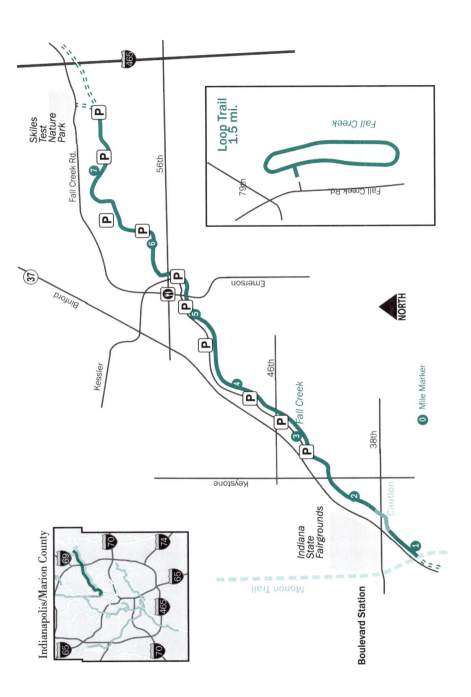

Monon Trail & Monon Greenway

Trail Uses	
Vicinity	Indianapolis, Carmel
Trail Length	15.7 miles total
	10.5 miles in Indy & 5.2 miles in Carmel
Surface	Asphalt
County	Marion, Hamilton

Trail Notes   The Monon Trail trail goes from 10th to 96ths Street, where it connects with the 5.2 mile Monon Greenway of Carmel. The Greenway continues north from 96th Street to 146th Street. This is one of the Midwest's most successful rail-trails in terms of popularity and design. The Monon links commercial districts, schools, parks, the state fairgrounds, and many residential neighborhoods. It connects to the Fall Creek Trail and the Central Canal Towpath. The Monon is quiet, wooded and tree-lined, without intersections north of 136th Street. The popular 146th Street sidepath, at the north end of the trail, runs east and west between Spring Mill Roads and SR37 in Noblesville.

There are plans to extend the trail northward from 146th Street to SR332, and then on to Sheridan. Several miles of new trails are planned between 116th and 111th Streets in Central Park.

Getting There   From downtown Canal Walk, take St. Clair Ave. west to Dorman. Proceed north on Dorman to 10th Street, then west to the trailhead just east of the Hwy 65/70 connection.

96th Street Trailhead – Take 96th Street east from US 31 for about a mile. The trailhead is on the north side of 96th Street. Restrooms and water are also available here.

Rohrer Road Trailhead – From 146th Street, turn south on Rohrer Road for about a half mile. There is trail parking on the left with restroom and water.

Depot Trailhead – From US 31, take Range Line Road south toward Carmel. Turn right at 131st Street (Main Street). Take the next left (south), and then right at the next block. You'll find trail parking and water on the left.

Contact Indianapolis Parks & Recreation   317-327-7431
Carmel-Clay Parks & Recreation   317-848-7275

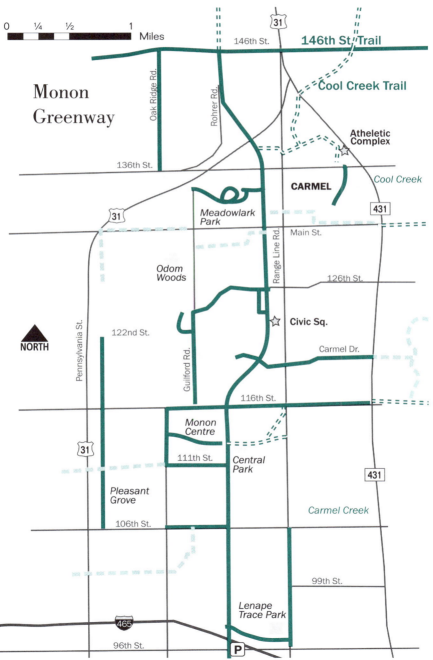

Monon Trail & Monon Greenway (continued)

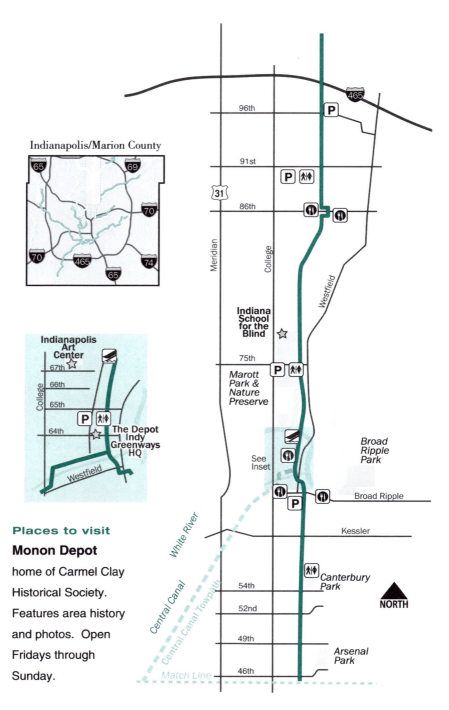

Places to visit

Monon Depot home of Carmel Clay Historical Society. Features area history and photos. Open Fridays through Sunday.

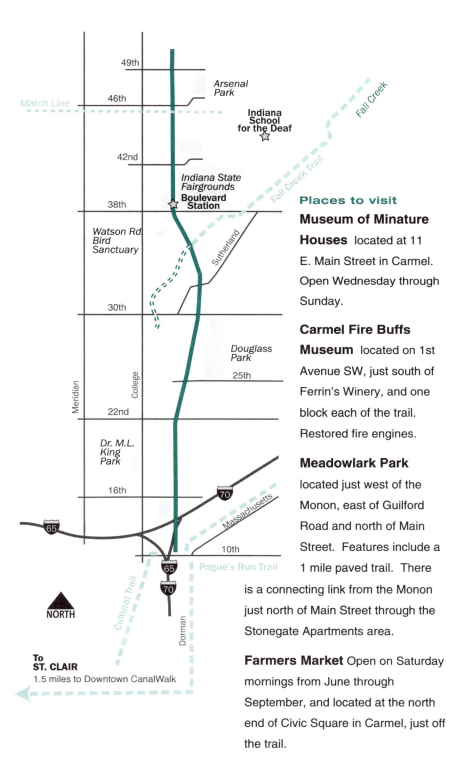

Places to visit

Museum of Minature Houses located at 11 E. Main Street in Carmel. Open Wednesday through Sunday.

Carmel Fire Buffs Museum located on 1st Avenue SW, just south of Ferrin's Winery, and one block each of the trail. Restored fire engines.

Meadowlark Park located just west of the Monon, east of Guilford Road and north of Main Street. Features include a 1 mile paved trail. There is a connecting link from the Monon just north of Main Street through the Stonegate Apartments area.

Farmers Market Open on Saturday mornings from June through September, and located at the north end of Civic Square in Carmel, just off the trail.

Owen-Putnam State Forest

Trail Uses

Vicinity   Spencer

Trail Length   14 miles

Surface   Natural

County   Owen, Putnam

Trail Notes   The Owen-Putnam State Forest is located in south central Indiana. The setting is hardwood forest through beautiful hills with views of a 50 foot sandstone bluff. Effort level is moderate to difficult. Mountain biking is only permitted on the designated areas of the Blue Horse Trail, which is shared with horseback riders. The trail is marked with blue decals. These markers are located on the right side of the trail until you pass the loop's halfway point, and then they continue on the left side. There are no trail use fees. Facilities include camping and picnic areas. Native wildlife species such as turkey, raccoon, deer, and fox are common to the area.

Getting There   Travel north on CR 400 West (Fish Creek Road) to the intersection of Atkinsonville Road (some 5 miles north of Hwy 46). Turn west (left) on Atkinsonville Road and go about ¾ miles to the trailhead parking lot located on the north side of the road. The parking lot has a 6 to 8 car capacity.

Contact   Owen-Putnam State Forest   812-829-2462

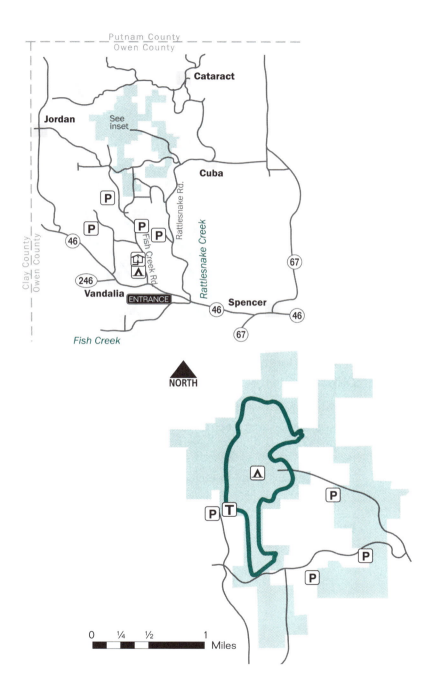

Pleasant Run Trail

Trail Uses

Vicinity Indianapolis

Trail Length 7 miles

Surface Asphalt

County Marion

Trail Notes The Pleasant Run Trail, 7 miles long and asphalt surfaced 5 to 12 feet wide, connects Garfield, Orange, Christian and Ellenberger community parks. Much of the trail runs along Pleasant Run stream and the roadway of the same name. The southern end of the trail is in the northwest corner of Garfield Park, near the intersection of Raymond Street and Pleasant Run Parkway. Ellenberger Park is located at the northeast end of the trail at Michigan Street and Pleasant Run Parkway. Some of the trail surface inside Ellenberger Park is crushed limestone.

Pleasant Run meanders as it travels through local neighborhoods. Generally the surface is flat with both shaded and open areas. Around English and Southeastern Avenues at its midsection, and again around Keystone Avenue, the trail follows narrow sidewalks with irregular surfaces, and crosses busy streets.

Getting There There are numerous access points. Off street parking is available in Garfield, Christian and Ellenberger Parks.

Contact Indianapolis Parks & Recreation 317-327-7431

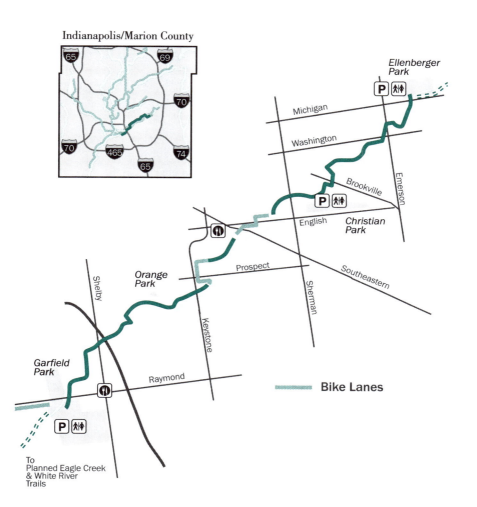

Pogue's Run Trail

Trail Uses	🚵 🏃
Vicinity	Indianapolis
Trail Length	4.0 miles, plus another 5 miles planned
Surface	Crushed limestone
County	Marion

Trail Notes   Pogue's Runs serves as a vital link in the Indy Greenways system. The trail was created to weave together Brookside and Spades Park, with the 1.5 miles Basin Trail anchoring as the corridor's north end. This is a 40 acre wetland and flood control project. The lower portions of Pogue's Run flows through concrete aqueducts beneath downtown Indianapolis. It passes through some of the oldest neighborhoods on Indianapolis' east side, including Woodruff Place and Cottage Home. Future development plans include a pathway through neighborhoods to the Monon Trail and the rest of the Indy Greenway trail system. The trail offers dramatic vistas of wetlands within an urban setting. Most of the trail surface is crushed stone.

Getting There   The Basin Trail trailhead and parking is located off Deuincy Avenue just west of 21st Street. Parking is also available in Brookside Park with access off Sherman Avenue, west of 16th Street.

Contact   Indianapolis Parks & Recreation   317-327-7431

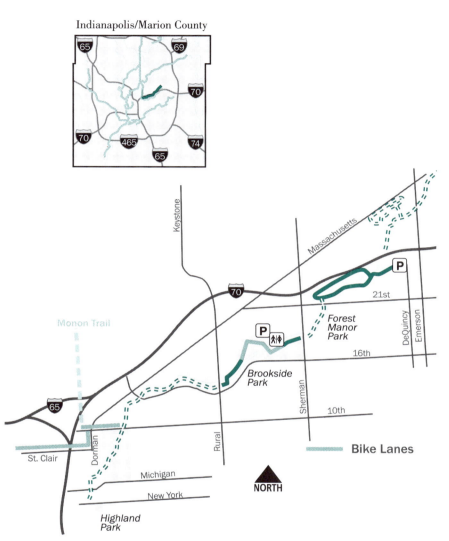

Sugar Creek Community Trail

Trail Uses	🚴 🚶 ⛸
Vicinity	Crawfordsville
Trail Length	4.5 miles
Surface	Asphalt
County	Montgomery

Trail Notes Sugar Creek Trail is a rail-trail located in Crawfordsville. It begins at the rear of Crawfordsville High School and travels along Grant Avenue to Indiana 32W, then westward to the east edge of the R.R. Donnelley & Company, where it heads into a natural woods area, emerging at 1100 Big Four Arch Road at the RR. Donnelley Trailhead Park. From there it follows Big Four Arch Road to Schenk Road. There it picks up the abandoned railroad and heads west to Sugar Creek. There are plans to extend the trail a half mile to reach a 40 acre wooded property to be known as Bigg's Bluff, which will be developed into mountain biking trails.

Restroom and water facilities can be found at the Crawfordsville High School, the Rock River Trailhead at 2722 W. Rock River Ridge Road, and the Crawfordsville Community Center at 922 E. South Blvd. The trail is open daily during daylight hours.

Getting There Crawfordville is located in west central Indiana, at the junction of Hwy 231, 47 and 74. Crawfordsville High School is located at 1 Athenian Drive off SR47 South.

Contact Crawfordville Parks & Recreation 765-364-5175

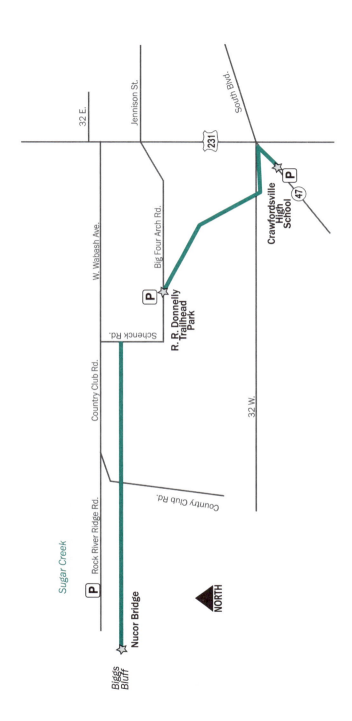

Town Run Trail Park

Trail Uses	
Vicinity	Indianapolis
Trail Length	9 miles
Surface	Packed dirt
County	Marion

Trail Notes   The Town Run Trail, also known as River's Edge Trail, is located on the far north side of Marion County, on the west side of White River, just south of 96th Street. The trail was developed and is maintained by the Hoosier Mountain Bike Association. Effort level on this single track, packed dirt trail is easy to moderate. It runs through wooded land on rolling terrain with several sharp twists and turns, plus some short but steep climbs and descents. The trail is marked with orange arrows and should be ridden clockwise. Operational hours are from dawn to dusk. There are plans to extend the park along the east side of White River from 82nd Street to north of 96th Street in Hamilton County.

The northern trailhead is located at the southwest corner of 96th Street and White River, between Keystone Avenue and Allisonville Road. The southern trailhead is located behind Bicycle Garage Indy North, on the north side of 82nd Street, between Keystone Avenue and Allisonville Road in Clearwater Crossing.

Getting There   From I-465 and Keystone Avenue, take Exit 33 south to Keystone Avenue for a half mile to 82nd Street. Proceed east on 82nd Street for a mile to the River's Edge Shopping Center parking lot on the east end next to the Bicycle Garage.

Contact   Town Run Trail Park 317-327-7431

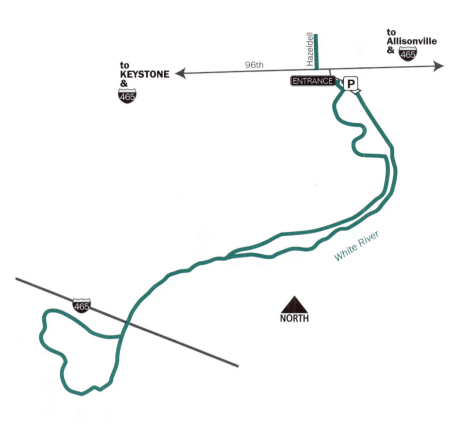
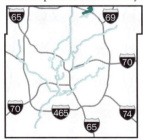

Westwood Park

Trail Uses	🚵 🚶 🔊
Vicinity	New Castle
Trail Length	10 miles
Surface	Natural
County	Henry

Trail Notes   Westwood Park is located in New Castle, less than an hour due east of downtown Indianapolis. The trail forms a complete loop around the lake and travels in a counter-clockwise direction starting across the road from the parking lot. Effort level is moderate with a number of short climbs of 25 to 30 feet. The setting is woodlands, rolling hills, and grasslands. The park's main attraction is the 180-acre lake. You'll be able to enjoy some great views of this beautiful lake along the ride. There are a couple of shared horse trail sections of about 100 yards each. The park is open year round. Facilities include a small modern campground, picnic area, playgrounds, and a shelter house.

Getting There   From Carmel or the north side of Indianapolis take 56th Street east to SR 67 (Pendleton Pike). Take a left on Pendleton Pike for about 4+ miles to McCordsville. From McCordsville, go right onto SR 234 for some 20 miles to Kennard. In Kennard, pick up CR 200 S for 5 miles to CR 400 W. Take CR 400 north (left) for a short distance to CR 175 S. Turn east (right) to CR 275 S. Continue on CR 275 S for a half mile to the park entrance.

From the south side of Indianapolis, take I-70 east to the New Castle/Spiceland exit (#123)). Go north into New Castle, and then west (left) on CR 200 S until it ends at Greensboro Pike. Take a left on Greensboro Pike to CR 275 W. Turn right on 275 W and continue around the lake to the park entrance.

Contact	Big River Conservancy District	765-9871232

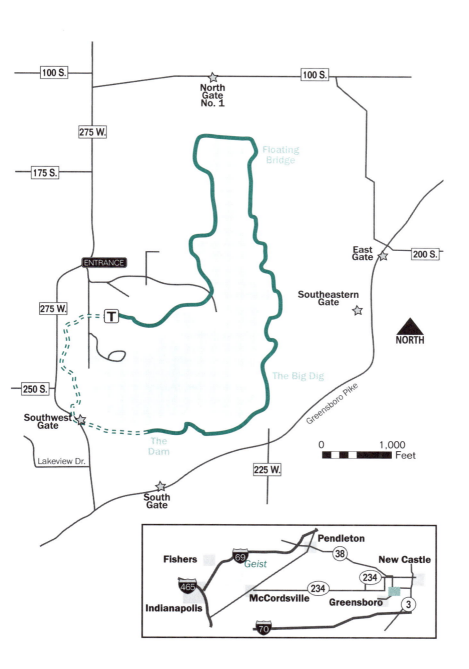

White River Wapahani Trail

Trail Uses

Vicinity Indianapolis

Trail Length 6.8 miles

Surface Asphalt

County Marion

Trail Notes The White Wapahani Trail runs from 38th Street south to White River State Park. Current development and plans will expand the trail to 8.3 miles. It now links with the Central Canal Towpath, the southern segment of the Fall Creek Trail, and the Downtown Canal Walk. Plans will take it to nearly the Johnson County Line. It will eventually link to the Eagle Creek Trails and the Pleasant Run Trail. There is a new section of the trail under construction on the top of the levee along Riverview Drive, between Kessler Blvd. and College Avenue.

Wapahani is the native name for the White River, and is the longest greenway in Marion County. It follows a winding path through the city from the northeast corner to the southwest. Platforms overlook the White River from the northwest corner of Broad Ripple Park and from the southeast corner of Meridian Street and Arden Avenue.

Getting There There are a number of access points along the trail. Parking is available near the southern trailhead at White River State Park, and at Riverside Park, Riverside Marina and the Major Taylor Velodrome.

Contact Indianapolis Parks & Recreation   317-327-7431

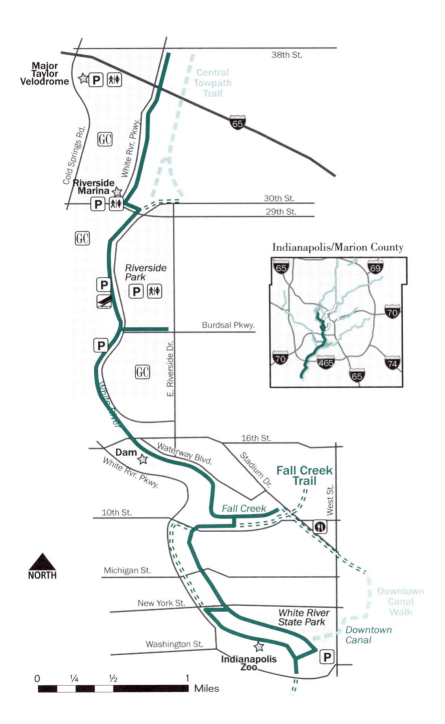

Southern Indiana

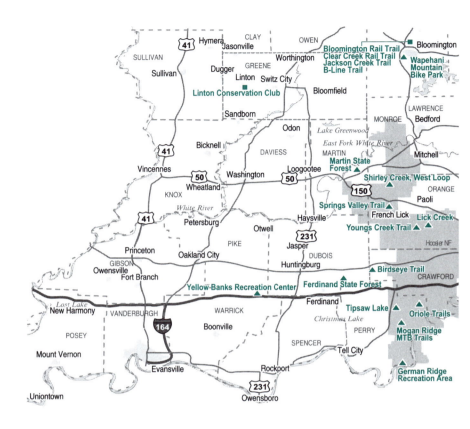

Trail Name	Page No.
Birdseye Trail	96
Bloomington's Trails	98
Brown County State Park	100
Clark State Forest	104
Ferdinand State Forest	106
German Ridge Recreation Area	108
Gnaw Bone Camp	110
Hickory Ridge Recreation Area	112
Jackson-Washington State Forest	116
Lick Creek Trail	118
Linton Conservation Club	120

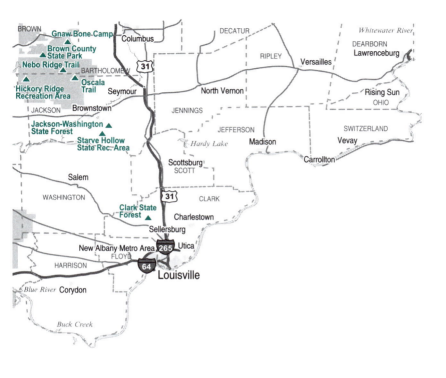

Trail Name	Page No.
Martin State Forest	122
Mogan Ridge Trail West	124
Nebo Ridge Trail	126
Ogala Trail	128
Oriole Trail – West & East	131
Shirley Creek Trail	134
Springs Valley Trail	136
Starve Hollow State Recreation Area	138
Tipsaw Lake Trail	140
Wapahani Mountain Bike Park	142
Yellow Banks Recreation Area	144
Youngs Creek Trails	146

Birdseye Trail
(Hoosier National Forest)

Trail Uses

Vicinity Birdseye, Marengo

Trail Length 12 miles

Surface Singletrack, fire road

County Orange

Trail Notes Two loops make up this trail - a 6 mile single track loop, marked by small blue arrows, and a 6 mile fire road loop. Effort level is moderate for the singletrack loop and easy for the fire road. The trail winds through a variety of terrain including hardwood forest, pine forest, and meadows. You will face some steep, technical climbs, rocky sections, a stream crossing, and long rolling hills. The trail tends to get overgrown with dense brush in the summer months, which adds to the challenge. Along the route are a lake, old homesteads, and a cemetery. Equestrians are required to have a permit.

Getting There Birdseye Trail is located about 40 miles west of Louisville. From I-64, take Hwy 145 north to Birdseye. Turn right on the gravel road that runs along the south side of the railroad tracks. After about a mile turn right (south) at the T intersection for a ¼ mile to a gate where you can park. The gate serves as the trailhead.

Contact Tell City Ranger District   812-547-6144

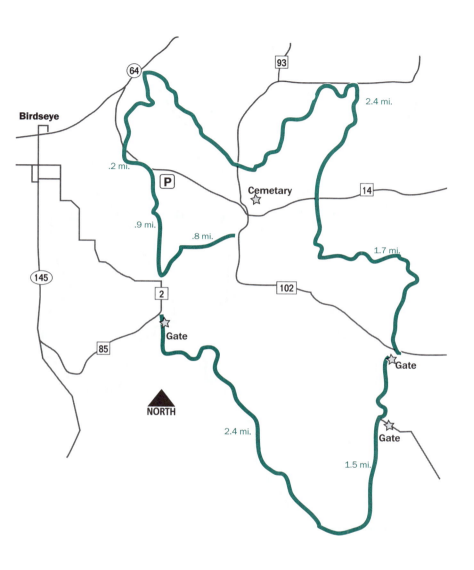

Bloomington's Trails

Bloomington Rail-Trail
Clear Creek Rail-Trail
Jackson Creek Trail
B-Line Trail

Trails	Trail Uses	Trail Length	Surface
Bloomington Rail Trail	🚲 🚶	2 miles	Crushed stone
Clear Creek Rail Trail	🚲 🚶 ⛸	2.3 miles	Asphalt
Jackson Creek Trail	🚲 🚶 ⛸	12 miles planned	Asphalt
B-Line Trail	🚲 🚶 ⛸	3 miles planned	Asphalt

Vicinity Bloomington

County Monroe

Trail Notes Plans call for the Bloomington Rail-Trail to be extended northward from Country Club road, curving west to Adams Street, an additional 3 miles into the heart of downtown Bloomington. The Clear Creek Trail will also eventually connect to Jackson Street Creek to the east, where another trail is planned along the creek. The first phases of the Jackson Creek Trails will be the area of Sherwood Oak Park and Childs elementary. Plans also include extending the Bloomington Rail-Trail southward past Dillman Road.

Planned B-Line Trail development phases:

Adams Street to Fairview Street – Ninth Street/Crestmont Park District
Fairview Street to Roger Street – Near West side District
Rogers Street to Second Street – Downtown District
Second Street to Grimes Lane – Seminary Square District
Grimes Lane to Country Club Drive – McDoel Switchyard District

Getting There Bloomington Rail Trail – Parking and access is available off Country Club Drive and Church Lane.

Clear Creek Trail – To get to the northern trailhead from downtown Bloomington take College Avenue south for 0.7 miles to Walnut Street. Go south on Walnut Street for 1.5 miles to Country Club Road. Take a right for a quarter mile to the parking area by the Bloomington Parks & Recreations building.

Contact Bloomington Parks & Recreation   812-349-3700

Photos courtesy of the Bloomington Parks & Recreation Department

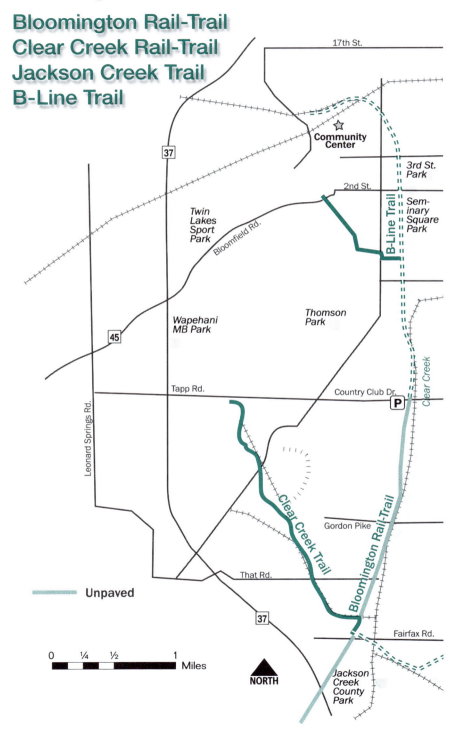

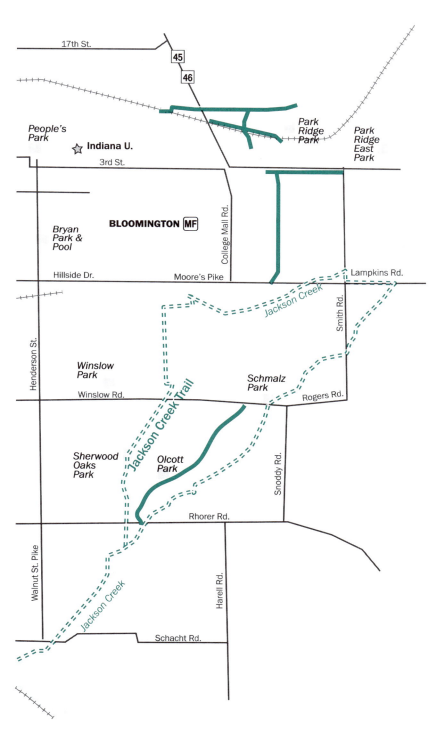

Brown County State Park

Trail Uses	
Vicinity	Nashville, IN
Trail Length	10 miles
Surface	Natural
County	Brown

Trail Notes   Brown County State Park is Indiana's largest state park, located in the Hoosier National Forest in south-central Indiana. It is the most visited park in the state, with fall during the leaf changing season being the most popular. The park covers almost 15,700 acres, and includes the 17 acre Ogle Lake and the 7 acre Strahl Lake. The Hoosier Mountain Bike Association (HMBA) has been active in maintaining and improving these mountain biking trails. In addition there are some 70 miles of bridle trails and 12 miles of hiking trails. The park provides a number of vistas that overlook wide swaths of deciduous forest.

Park facilities include camping, cabins, shelters, a lodge, swimming pool, Nature Center, and a rental and recreation building. Nashville is known for its summer-stock theater and antique shops.

Getting There   From Indianapolis, take I-65 south to SR 46. Exit west (right) onto SR46, past SR135 South to the entrance road on the left. Cross a covered bridge and go past the gatehouse. Take a right where the road divides to a parking area on your right.

Contact   Brown County State Park   812-988-6406

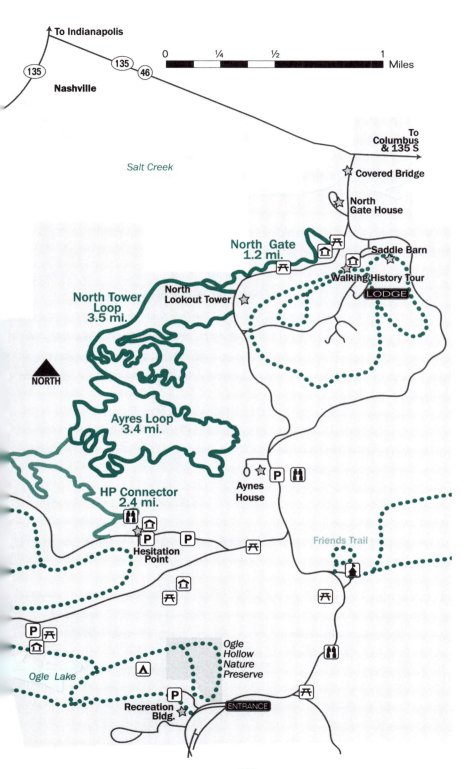

Clark State Forest

Trail Uses	
Vicinity	Sellersburg, New Pekin
Trail Length	5 miles
Surface	Gravel, dirt
County	Clark

Trail Notes   The bike trails at the Deam Lake Complex Clark State Forest consists of 3.5 miles of fire lanes on the east side of the trails and 1.75 miles of wood trail on the west side. The east side is entirely gravel and mostly flat. Effort level is easy. The west side is gravel and dirt and somewhat hilly. There is also a spur on the northwest side of the trail that leads to the northern part of Deam Lake and a single track that winds through the woods, coming out near parking lot #3. There are several moderate hills on the west side, but no jumps or obstacles. Most of the climbs are followed by a level run.

Bikers share the trail with horseback riders, and mountain bikes are only permitted on the bike trails. The trail is marked with blue decals on Carsonite posts on the right side of the trail.

All three parking lots have accessible trailheads. Parking lot #1 is located past the entrance gate on Deam Lake. Parking lot #2 is located on Wilson Switch Road on the east side of the dam. The third lot is located east of Deam Lake and is accessible by taking Wilson Switch Road east a mile to Flower Gap, then turning left for a mile until the road turns into a fire lane. The lot is on the right.

Getting There   From Salem, take SR 60 southeast past New Providence and Borden Hill to Wagoner Knob Road. Go north on Wagoner Knob Road. Reference the illustrated trail map for the parking areas and trailheads.

Contact   Clark Forest & Deam Lake Complex   812-246-5421

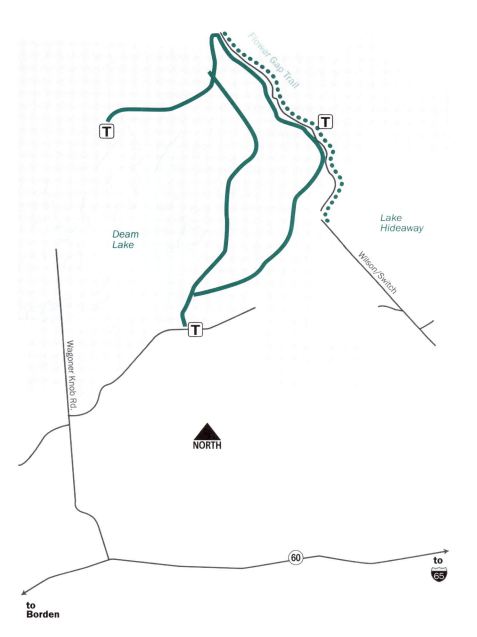

Ferdinand State Forest

Trail Uses	🏍️ 🚶
Vicinity	Ferdinand
Trail Length	8.8 miles
Surface	Natural, groomed
County	Dubois

Trail Notes There are five bike and hiking trails totaling 8.8 miles. They consist of partially wooded trails and wooded roads. The trails are marked with blue decals on Carsonite brand posts. They range in difficulty from moderate to difficult. You can expect some serious climbing. Bikers are not permitted to stray off the marked trails, but they may use the improved rock or paved property roads to make shorter loops.

The trails start at a double trailhead in the first parking lot on the right as you enter the forest property. The north trailhead starts the Foxey Hollow Trail, which travels north from the parking lot. It comes to an end at the intersection of the Firetower Trail and the Twin Lake Trail. Turning left allows you to stay on the Firetower Trail and turning right leads you through the large campground which loops around and connects to the Twin Lakes Trail. The Firetower Trail merges at the Firetower with the Kayana Trail. This trail loops around the northeast corner of the property and becomes the Twin Lakes Trail. The Twin Lakes Trail runs along the east side of the property.

Taking the south trailhead at the parking lot begins the South Ridge Trail. This trail runs along the south side of the property and merges with the Twin Lakes Trail on the southeast side by Fossil Lake.

Getting There From Ferdinand take SR162 for about a mile north to SR264 northeast to the Ferdinand State Forest entrance. The parking lot is on the right shortly after entering the park.

Contact Ferdinand State Forest 812-367-1524

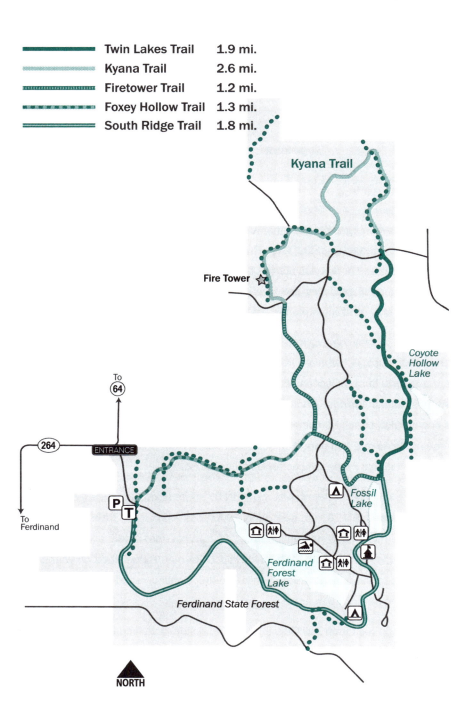

German Ridge Recreation Area

Trail Uses

Vicinity Derby, Tell City

Trail Length 24 miles

Surface Singletrack, gravel road

County Perry

Trail Notes The German Ridge Trail is a multiple loop trail consisting of singletrack and gravel roads that wind through sandstone rock outcrops, rolling hills of hardwood forests, and Ohio River views. The trails are open to mountain biking, hiking and horseback riding. They are posted with decals and colored dots or diamonds indicating use type. Blue is multi-use, yellow is mountain biking and hiking only, and white means open only to hiking.

Effort level is easy to moderate. The trails are laid out in a ladder style, for bigger or smaller loops. Climbs are frequent, and a few are difficult. The south end is a gravel lane through woods. Single track is found on the north end. There are some stream crossings. Facilities include a primitive campground with pit toilets, a scenic lake, beach and picnic shelter. Mountain bikers and horse riders are required to have a trail permit, either annual or day-use, and are available from Hoosier National Forest offices and local vendors.

Getting There From I-64, go to IN 37 south (Exit 79). Take IN 37 south about 18 miles to IN 70. Go east on IN 70 for less than a mile, then turn right to the big "German Ridge Recreation Area" sign. When that road T's into another, turn right onto Gerald Road. When you reach German Ridge Road on your left, turn and go to the parking area 0.9 miles south. Continue south to reach the campground and day use area.

From I-66, go east from Tell City, through Cannelton, watching for Forest Service signs. From there, go north on German Ridge Road. The campground and trailhead is approximately ¾ of a mile further to the left.

Contact Tell City Ranger District 812-547-7051

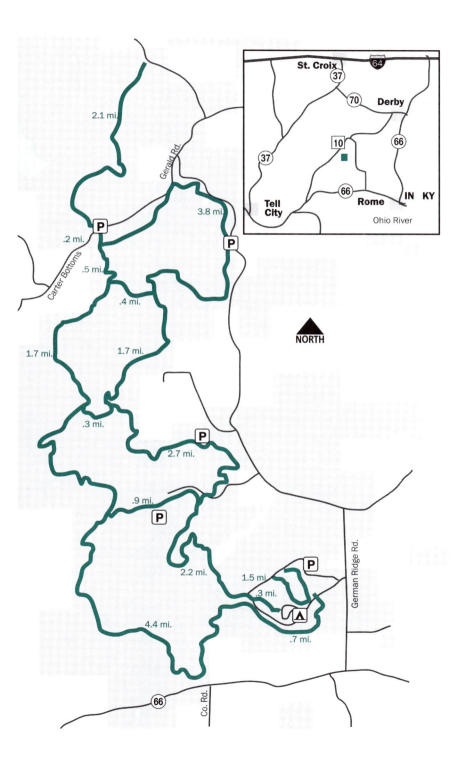

Gnaw Bone Camp

Trail Uses	
Vicinity	Nashville, IN
Trail Length	25 miles
Surface	Natural, groomed
County	Brown

Trail Notes Gnaw Bone Camp provides over 25 miles of marked woods trails for mountain biking. The trails are groomed and range from easy to difficult. Some of the climbs are challenging with steep, technical descents. You will also experience stream crossings, fast downhills, slate rock, and wooden bridges. There is a $3 entrance fee and a liability release to be signed. It is open daily, but you should call in advance as the camp may be leased out or it is too wet (812-988-6638). Follow the blue trail markers, but if you get confused backtrack or go to a blacktop road. Stay off trails not identified on the map.

Getting There Take I-65 to SR46 near Columbus. Go west about 10 miles to SR135. Take SR135 south for about 2 miles to Gnawbone Camp, just past Shepherd Road. Turn east (left) into the camp and park at the General Store.

Contact Gnawbone Camp   812-988-6638

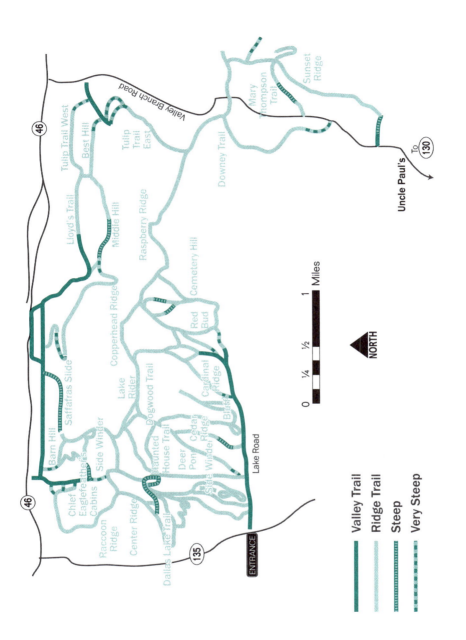

Hickory Ridge Recreation Area

Trail Uses

Vicinity   Bloomington, Norman Station

Trail Length   46 miles

Surface   Singletrack, fire roads

County   Jackson

Trail Notes   Hickory Ridge is located in the Hoosier National Forest southeast of Bloomington. The trails consist of a series of long and short interweaving loops through hardwood forests. They are well marked with signs at intersections. Effort level ranges from easy to difficult. The ridgetops tend to be easier riding, while the ravines are more difficult. The trails are designated multiple-use. Facilities include a primitive campground with pit toilets for horse camping, but day use parking is also available. Bring your own food and water.

Horse riders and mountain bikers are required to have a trail permit, either annual or day-use. These permits are available from Hoosier National Forest offices and local vendors. Horseback riding is common near the parking area, but more infrequent as you ride further out.

Getting There   From Hwy 446 turn east on Hwy 58 East. Proceed 6.5 miles to Norman. Turn left at the brown FS sign. Continue another 0.3 miles and turn left onto CR1250 West at a brown FS sign.   Take CR 1250 for 1.5 miles to Hickory Grove Road. Turn right when you see a another brown FS sign and continue another 0.7 miles to Hickory Ridge Trailhead on the left side of the road.

Contact   Brownstown Ranger District   812-275-5987

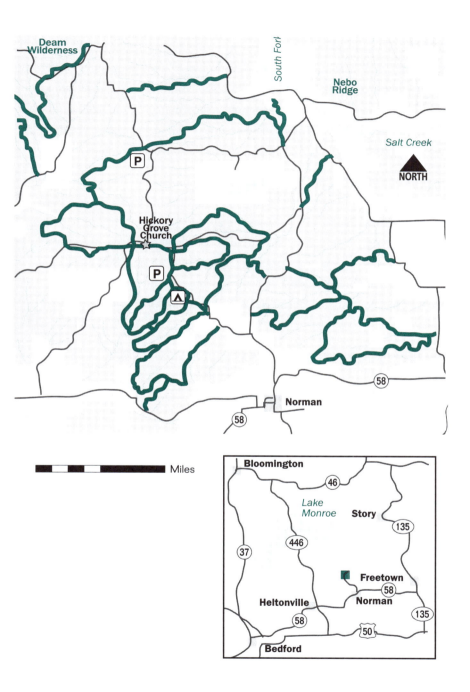

Hoosier National Forest

The Hoosier National Forest, totaling approximately 200,000 acres, is located in the rolling hills of southern Indiana. This is south of where the glaciers stopped their advance, and melt waters carved out valleys and left sharp ridges. Where ancient shallow seas once stood, limestone is undercut with subterranean rivers, and the land is dotted with springs, caves, and sinkholes.

The National Forest is within a two hour drive of Evansville, Indianapolis, Cincinnati, and Louisville. You can access it north-south by SR 37, and east-west by US 50 and I-64. These lands are available for biking, hiking, horseback riding, camping, hunting, and fishing. State hunting and fishing licenses are required. Be aware this National Forest is interspersed with private land. For current information on sites, trail information, rules and regulations, and accessibility, contact the Hoosier National Forest office in Bedford at 812-275-5987.

The following sites open to biking are included in this publication:

Birdseye Trail
German Ridge Trail
Hickory Ridge Trail
Lick Creek Trail
Mogan Ridge West Trail
Nebo Ridge Trail
Ogala Trail
Oriole Trail - East & West
Shirley Creek Trail
Tipsaw Trail
Youngs Creek Trail

Photos courtesy of Hoosier National Forest

Jackson-Washington State Forest

Trail Uses

Vicinity Brownstown

Trail Length 8.8 miles

Surface Singletrack, fireroads

County Jackson, Washington

Trail Notes Jackson-Washington State Forest encompasses more than 17,000 acres in the heart of southern Indiana, and is within two miles of Starve Hollow State Recreation Area. The Forest contains a unique topography known as the "Knobs Region". There are three loop trails, each identified with a different color – blue, green, and orange. These trails are shared with horses. Bike decals posted on the right indicate that you are leaving the parking area. The letter P for parking lot will be on a brown post when you reach the halfway point of a loop to indicate that you are heading back to the parking lot. Effort level is moderate to difficult and demanding, with constant climbs and descents. Many of the climbs head directly up the hills, without benefit of switchbacks. The downhills are frequently laden with rocks and ruts. Wet weather can make these trails near impossible.

Camping, water and other facilities are available at the Starve Hollow State Recreation area.

Getting There From Brownstown on Hwy 50, head south on 50 W to the trailhead and parking just north of the junction with 340 S.

Contact Jackson-Washington State Forest   812-358-2160

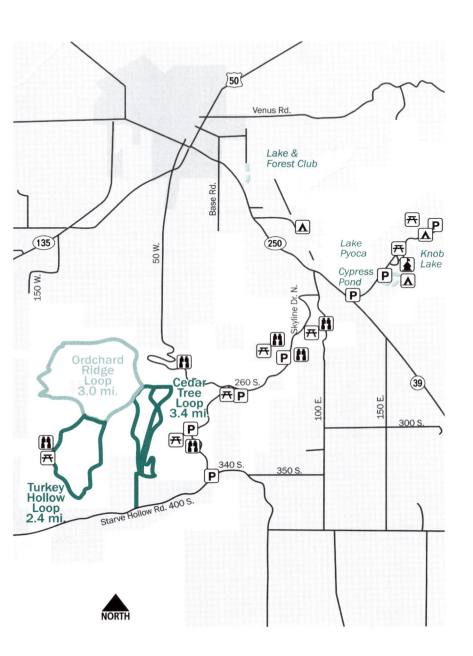

Lick Creek Trail

Trail Uses	🚵 🚶 ⌒
Vicinity	Paoli
Trail Length	7.5 miles
Surface	Singletrack, service road
County	Orange

Trail Notes This loop trail passes through scenic hardwood forest and rolling hills. Effort level is easy to moderate, with a few short climbs and descents. In the early 19th century the area, known locally as 'Little Africa', served as a free African American settlement. Only a family cemetery and traces of home sites remain. It is open daily, and there is a small entrance fee.

The trail is posted with decals and colored coded with dots or diamonds. Blue is open for multi-use. Yellow is mountain biking and hiking only. White is hiking only. The connector trail from the parking area to the loop is 1.7 miles, and the connector from Grease Gravy Road to the loop is a half mile. The loop is approximately 5.2 miles long.

Getting There From Paoli, follow IN37 for 5.3 miles to CR 450 South. A sign for Marengo Cave marks the intersection. Turn left on CR450, and follow it for one mile to the Lick Creek parking area. Turn left into the parking area. The trailhead is located on the east end.

Contact Tell City Ranger District 812-547-7051

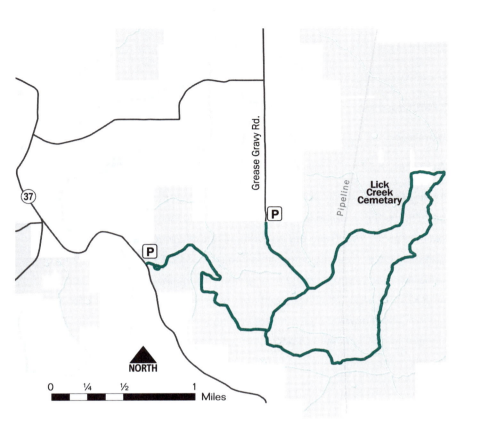
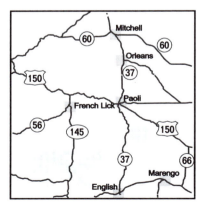

Linton Conservation Club

Trail Uses

Vicinity   Linton

Trail Length   4 miles

Surface   Singletrack, dirt roads

County   Greene

Trail Notes   Linton's trails were developed on a reclaimed stripmining pit. The setting is rolling terrain. These are really just mounds, produced from old mining activity. There are no major climbs or descents. Effort level is generally easy. The ride carries you through short pitches, with the momentum generated carrying you up the next climb. This mountain biking park got its start in 1993 when Jay Gainey and Mike Murphy approached the Linton City Council about developing a mountain biking trail on neglected land behind the Conservation Club that was becoming a dumping ground. They agreed to clear the land and cut the trails with the understanding that mountain biking be allowed.

Getting There   From Bloomington, take Hwy 37 to Hwy 45 South. Follow Hwy 45 for 14 miles to Hwy 445. Take Hwy 445 west for 4 miles to Hwy 54, and then west of Hwy 54 for approximately 26 miles to Linton. In Linton, take a right (west) onto CR100 for about a mile to the Linton Conservation Club and parking lot.

From the parking lot, the trail starts up the gravel road to the right just past the toilets. Here you have a choice of two trails. The one up the hill to the left is the longer of the two, but they both intersect each other several times.

Contact   Bicycle Garage, Bloomington
                     812-339-3457

                     Linton-Stockton Chamber of Commerce
                     812-847-4846

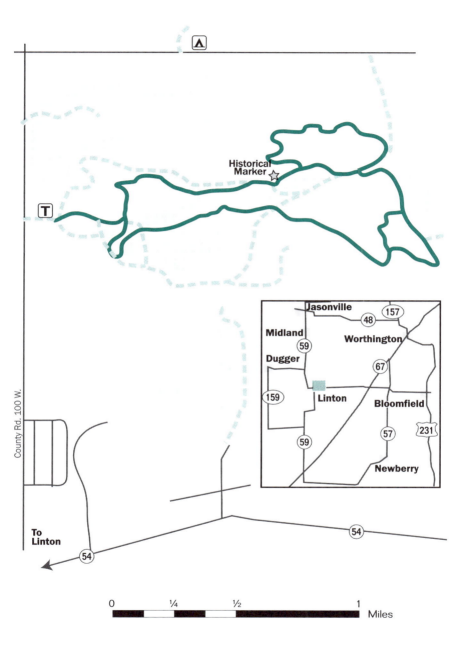

Martin State Forest

Trail Uses	🚵 🚶
Vicinity	Shoals
Trail Length	12 miles
Surface	Grass fire lanes, some crushed stone
County	Martin

Trail Notes   Marin State Forest contains 8,066 acres, and is a lush, healthy, and growing forest. The bike trail follows existing fire trails composed of a mix of fairly level ridgetops and slopes. Effort level is easy to moderate. There are 4 trails of which the main trail, at 5 miles, is the longest in length. The other three trails are connecting, allowing you to select shorter loops. Most of the hills have easy grades, and are fairly smooth. The trails are all grass except for the trailhead, which is gravel. All the trails are mowed at least twice a year to a minimum width of five feet, and are designed for two-way travel. The trails are marked with blue bike decals attached to Carsonite-brand posts on both sides of the trail. Mountain bikers are limited to marked trails with these blue decals. There are no trail use fees. You might want to call ahead to the park for trail conditions.

Facilities include picnic shelter and primitive camping with toilets and drinking water available. Three lakes are open to fishing – Martin Lake, Hardwood Lake, and Pine Lake. Hunting is allowed in season, so be aware that they are free to use the trails.

Getting There   Martin State Forest is located 20 miles southwest of Bedford, and 4 miles east of Shoals, on Hwy 50. The trailhead parking lot is located off of Forest Road. To get to the lot, take the forest's main entrance, on the north side of US 50, to Forest Road. Go to the left where the road forks. The parking lot is the second lane on the left side of the road across from the arboretum.

Contact   Martin State Forest   812-247-3491

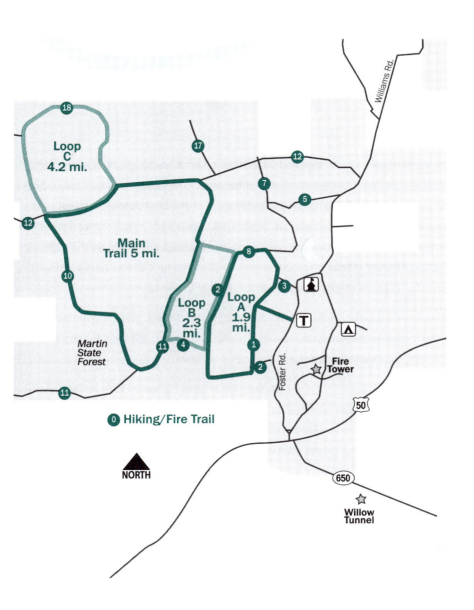

Mogan Ridge Trail West

Trail Uses	🚵 🚶 🐴
Vicinity	Tell City, Derby
Trail Length	12.5 miles
Surface	Singletrack, fire roads
County	Perry

Trail Notes   Mogan Ridge West offers a few tough climbs, and some fairly technical singletrack sections. Effort level is moderate. Two of the sections are singletrack with gravel road in between. For the best descents, travel counter-clockwise. The trails are shared with horseback riders and hikers. There is a trail permit fee, either day-use or annual. Permits are available from Hoosier National Forest offices and local vendors. The setting is scenic hardwood forests. Trails at Mogan Ridge East are limited to hikers.

The trails are posted with colored dot or diamond decals. Blue is open for multi-use. Yellow is only open to mountain biking and hiking. White is for hiking only. Parking is available, but there are no other facilities.

Getting There   From I-64, take IN 37 (Exit 79) south toward Tell City for about 18 miles to IN 70. Go east on IN 70 for a short distance to Old IN 37, then north of 1.1 miles to the Mogan Ridge sign on the right (east) side of the road. Take this unmarked gravel road for 0.4 miles to the radio tower parking are on the left.

Contact   Tell City Ranger District   812-547-7051

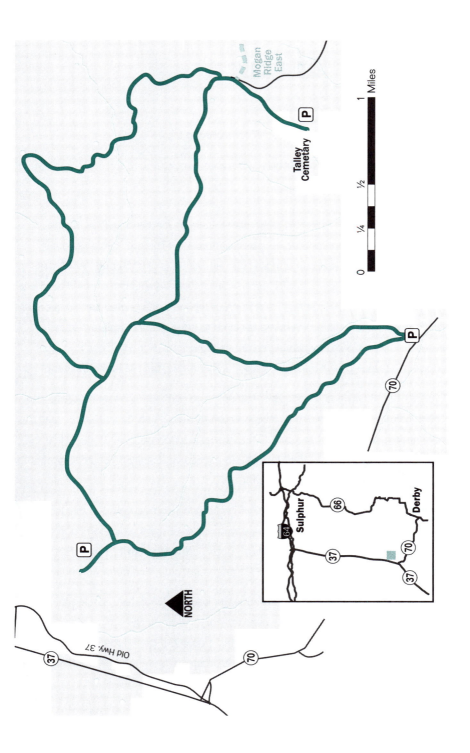

Nebo Ridge Trail

Trail Uses	
Vicinity	Story
Trail Length	8.5 miles (17 miles round trip)
Surface	Singletrack
County	Brown

Trail Notes   Nebo Ridge, also known as Knobstone Trail, is one of the most popular mountain biking trails in Indiana. The trail is roller coaster singletrack through woods and rocky hillsides, with lots of short and fast climbs and descents. The ride provides some scenic views from its ridge tops. There are trails connecting to this out and back trail, but they are designated for hiking only. Mountain biker and horse riders are required to have a trail permit, either daily or annual. Permits are available from Hoosier National Forest offices and local vendors. Camping is permitted in back-country areas, but not at the trailhead.

This is the only area of the Hoosier National Forest where visitors regularly see rattlesnakes. The timber rattler has a series of wide black cross-bands lining the back along the length of its body. They average in length from 48 to 72 inches with a rattle on the end of their tail. Avoid excessive activity if you are bitten, and seek medical care as soon as possible.

To hook up with nearby Hickory Ridge Trails at the southern end of this trail, turn right (west) onto CR 1000 N for about a mile. Take the first left once over a bridge. At the road intersection, turn (north) right onto Tower Ridge Road and follow it for about a half mile to Trail 20 on the left side, just before a bridge.

Getting There   From Columbus, go west on IN 46 for 13 miles to IN 135 south. Take SR 135 south for 9 miles to Story. Veer off SR 135 at the Story Inn (unmarked Elkinsville Road). Go 2.7 miles, passing a gravel road on your right. Take the left bend in the road and cross a bridge. Continue for 0.3 miles and then turn left into the parking area.

Contact	Brownstown Ranger District	812-275-5987
	Nebo Ridge Bicycles	317-471-1069

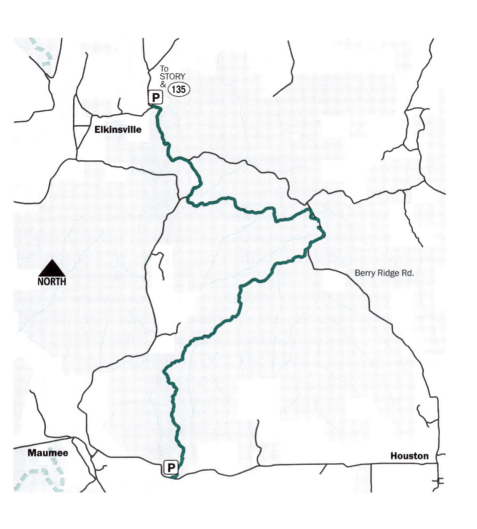
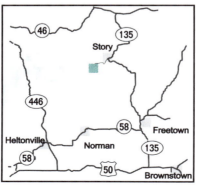

Ogala Trail

Trail Uses	🏍️ 🚶 🐴
Vicinity	Freetown, Bloomington
Trail Length	6 miles
Surface	Singletrack, forest and county roads
County	Jackson

Trail Notes There are some 6 miles of lowland multiple-use trail through scenic hardwood forest making up the Ogala Trail. The trail traverses some small ridges and ravines. Effort level is easy to moderate. One leg of the trail passes to the north of Sundance Lake, which was named after a Native American purification ceremony. Once past Sundance Lake, the gullies and the dirt road, the trail flattens out before continuing to some worthy climbs. Near the east end of the trail, you'll pass over a couple of ridges before returning to the west. User reports indicate the trail is in need of maintenance, and seems mostly undeveloped and poorly marked. There is a trail use fee, daily or annual. Permits are available from Hoosier National Forest offices and local vendor.

The trails are posted with colored dots or diamond decals. Blue is open to mountain biking, hiking and horse riding. Yellow is limited to mountain biking and hiking. White is only open to hiking.

The Ogala Trail is under consideration to be closed to bicyclists, so you may want to check the status before venturing there.

Getting There Take IN 46 west of Columbus or east of Nashville to IN 135 South. Take IN 135 south for 16.3 miles to CR 1190 North. This is the first road you can turn left on once you cross the Jackson County Line. Turn left on CR 1190 North for 1.1 mile as it bends to the right and left until you reach the gravel road parking area.

Contact Brownstown Ranger District   812-275-5987

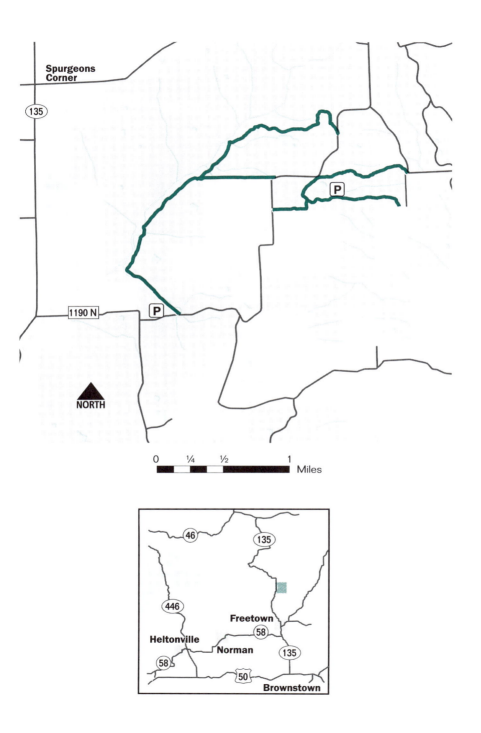

Photograph courtesy of Hoosier National Forest

Oriole Trails – West & East

Trail Uses	
Vicinity	Sulphur
Trail Length	Oriole West 7.2 miles
	Oriole East 10 miles
Surface	Singletrack, forest & gravel roads
County	Perry

Trail Notes   Both trails are located in the southern section of the Hoosier National Forest. Daily or annual trail use permits are required. They are available from Hoosier National Forest offices and local vendors. The trails are open daily, year round. The nearest public phone is located in Sulphur.

Oriole West

This multiple use trail takes you through hardwood forest, pasture and creeks. Effort level is moderate with some technical sections, and some interesting descents and climbs. The trails are mostly forest roads. Taking them counterclockwise is suggested for a better ride. Overall, the climbs are not numerous, and most descents are on easier grade.

Oriole East

Oriole East consists of two loops, one 7 miles long and the other 3 miles. Effort level is moderate with some tough climbs. As with Oriole West, going right on the main trail and the 3 mile loop on the east end is recommended. The setting is hardwood forest.

Getting There   **Oriole West** From I-64 to SR66 South through Sulphur for about 5 miles. Turn right on CR52, and continue west for a mile to the trailhead and parking area. **Oriole East** From I-64 take SR 37 west for four miles to Jeffries Cemetery. Look for a small Hoosier National Forest sign on the right side of the road. Turn left into the parking area next to the cemetery. Park there or go across the road to Oriole Pond.

Contact   Tell City Ranger District   812-547-7051

Oriole Trails – West

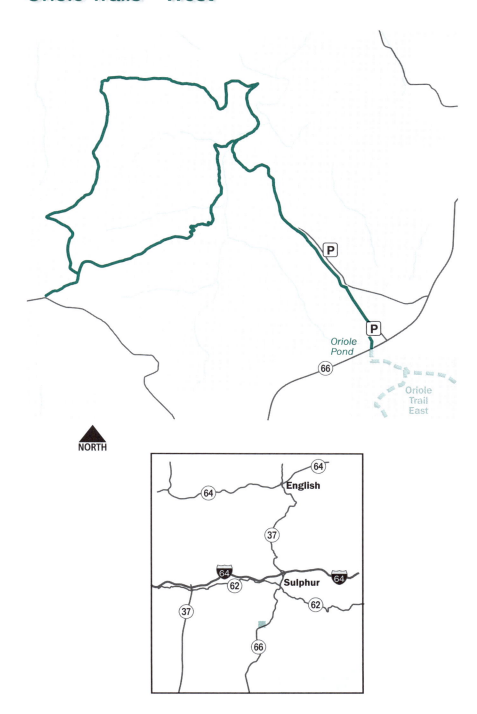

Oriole Trails – East

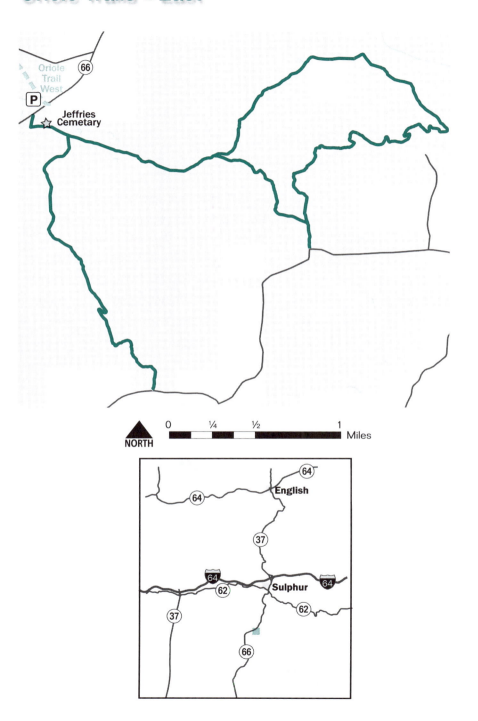

Shirley Creek Trail

Trail Uses	🚵 🚶 🐴
Vicinity	Orleans
Trail Length	19.5 miles
Surface	Singletrack
County	Orange

Trail Notes Shirley Creek Trail consists of several loops, providing many options. Effort level is generally moderate but can be demanding, with lots of hilly singletrack and occasional streambeds. Stay only on designated trails. These will be identified with colored posts with dots or decals. The terrain is scenic hardwood forest and often steep. You probably find some areas of the trail chewed up by horse hoofs. There is a primitive campground with pit toilets, but no fee for the campground. Mountain bikers and horse rider are required to have a trail permit, either daily or annual. Permits are available from Hoosier National Forest offices and local vendors.

Getting There Shirley Creek is located about 10 miles west of Orleans in northwest Orange County. From Bedford, take Hwy 50 west for 9.6 miles to the intersection of Hwys 50 and 60. Continue west on Hwy 50 for 0.1 miles to the county road on the left. Take this county road, cross some railroad tracks, and continue for 0.9 miles to CR 825 West. Take a right on CR 825 and go 3.4 miles to the split in the road where you turn left onto CR 810 North. Pass Bonds Chapel and a cemetery on the right, driving 1.3 miles to CR 775. Turn right on CR 775 and go 1.2 miles to the Shirley Creek Trail sign on the left. Follow the road to the trailhead and campground.

Contact Brownstown Ranger District 812-275-5987

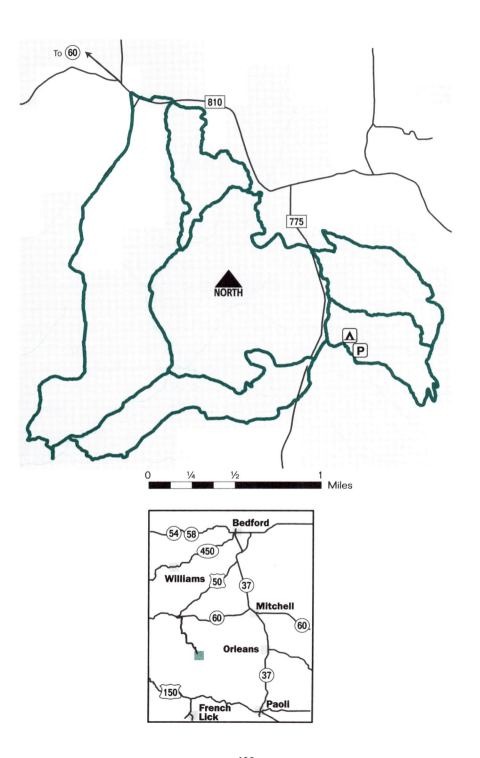

Springs Valley Trail

Trail Uses	🚵 🚶 🧲
Vicinity	Paoli, French Lick
Trail Length	12.7 miles
Surface	Double track, gravel roads
County	Orange

Trail Notes   Spring Valley, located in the Hoosier National Forest, consists of a loop trail around the lake and a one-way spur trail at the east end of the lake that heads east to CR 310 W. Effort level is easy to somewhat moderate. The ride area is mostly wooded with scenic views of the 140 acre Springs Valley Lake and remnants of the Buffalo Trace. The recreation area is located on the north shore of the lake where parking is available at the trailhead. Facilities include a campground, picnic area and restrooms, all found near the recreation area. No fees are charged for entry, parking, or use of the boat ramp, but mountain bikers and horse riders are required to have a trail permit and stay on trails designated for their use. The daily or annual permits are available from Hoosier National Forest offices and local vendors.

Getting There   From Hwy 37 south of Paoli, go west on CR 550 S/CR 560 S at Pine Valley, and continue west for about 0.8 miles. Turn right into the trailhead parking area by a FR 707 sign.

From Hwy 145 South out of French Lick, go 6.4 miles and turn left at the brown FS sign on Baseline Liberty Road. Continue for 4.8 miles to the trailhead on the left.

From Hwy 37 south of Paoli, turn right on Unionville Road for 1 mile. Turn right at the brown FS sign onto CR 150 South, and proceed 1.1 miles to a stop sign. Turn left onto CR 225 West for 2.1 miles to another brown FS sign and bear left onto County Road 325 West. Take CR 325 West for 4.9 miles to the Springs Valley Trailhead on the right side of the road.

Contact	Hoosier National Forest	812-275-5987

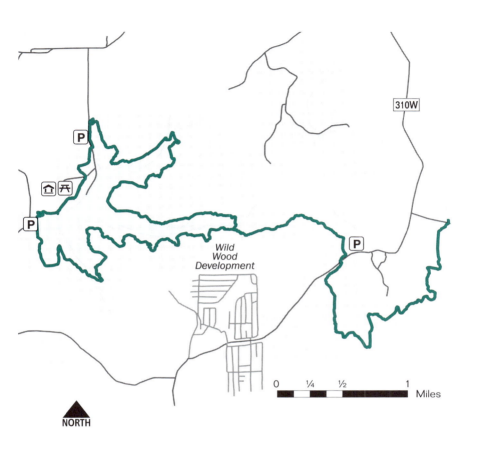
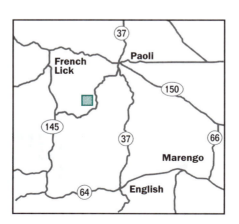

Starve Hollow State Recreation Area

Trail Uses

Vicinity   Brownstown

Trail Length   3.7 miles

Surface   Singletrack, fireroads

County   Jackson

Trail Notes   Starve Hollow Recreation Area is adjacent to Jackson-Washington State Forest and features a 145 acre lake. The trails provide scenic views of the lake. The rolling hills involve some steep climbs as you travel through the area's woodlands. Effort level is moderate. There are 5 trail sections ranging from one half to 1.3 miles, each with identifying color trail markers.

The Recreation Area provides large, modern campgrounds with electrical hookups, restrooms and showers. Other facilities include picnic tables, drinking water, a swimming beach, boat rental, play area, and the Driftwood Fish Hatchery.

Getting There   The Recreation Area is located southeast of Brownstown, 2 miles off Hwy 135 on CR275 West.

Contact   Starve Hollow State Recreation Area   812-358-3464

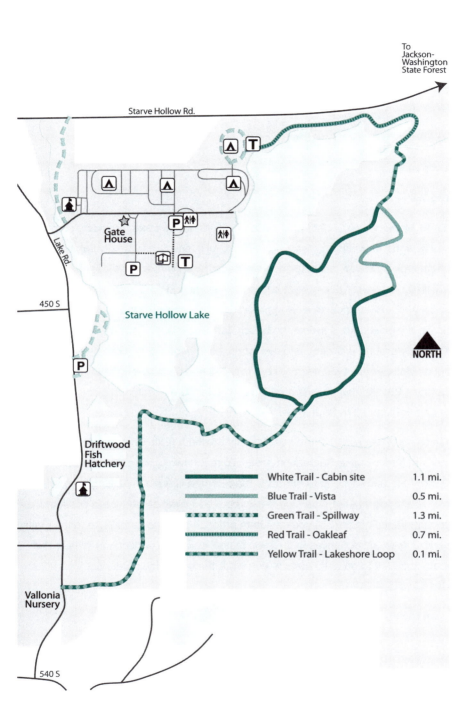

Tipsaw Lake Trail

Trail Uses	
Vicinity	Tell City, St. Croix
Trail Length	6 miles
Surface	Singletrack
County	Perry

Trail Notes The trail circles around Tipsaw Lake, providing some scenic and memorable views. The effort level is easy. It is mostly flat with some rocky areas, shallow ravines, climbs, and a few moderate climbs. You will also experience a couple of stream crossings and a frequently muddy section. Facilities include a campground, group camps, picnic sites and shelters overlooking the lake, a swimming beach, boat rentals, and a modern bathhouse. The campground is divided into two loops, each containing drinking water, flush toilets, and hot showers. There is a day use parking fee (from April 1 thru October 15). Annual passes are also available. The beach and picnic area is open from May 23 to September 15.

Getting There From I-64, take IN 37 south (Exit 79) approximately 6.5 miles to Tipsaw Lake Recreation Area. To reach two of the parking areas, turn right on the recreation area entrance road. There is a small parking area prior to the gatehouse where no parking fee is required. If the gatehouse is occupied, a parking fee is required. If you decide to proceed past the gatehouse to the main parking area, drive 3 miles to the swimming/picnic area parking lot. Where the road curbs left to go to the beach, you'll see the trail going right, past a pit toilet and into the woods.

Contact Tell City Ranger District   812-547-7051

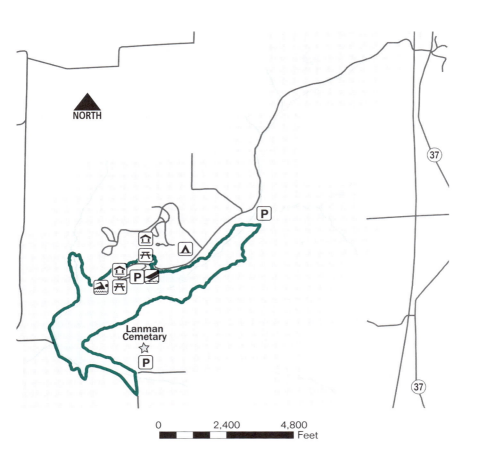
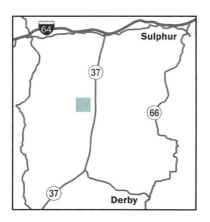

Wapehani Mountain Bike Park

Trail Uses

Vicinity   Bloomington

Trail Length   9 miles

Surface   Singletrack

County   Monroe

Trail Notes   The Wapehani Mountain Bike Park took root in 1990. It was developed with the help of volunteers who cleaned up the site and built trails after the Boy Scouts moved out in 1980 and the property became an unauthorized dump site. This 34 acre wood park is located off of Weimer Road, between West Second Street and Tapp Road in Bloomington. It is well maintained. There are two entrances to the trail system from the parking lot. The one with the large gate leads to the lake loop. There are two hills on the other side of the lake that are short but extremely steep and challenging.

The park contains a network of moderate to more difficult trails. There are some steep climbs and descents through woods, even some jumps, and a loop around a lake offering views of beautiful scenery. You'll find lots of ruts, steep hard turns, large root systems, large log to hop, creeks to cross, and wooden slat/log bridges to keep you in prime condition.

Getting There   From Hwy. 37 near Bloomington, take 2nd Street east to Weimer Road. Turn right on Weimer Road and continue to Rock Road (West Wapehani Road). Go right on Rock Road for about a quarter mile to the parking area.

From Bloomington, take 2nd Street west to Weimer Road. Take Weimer Road left for 0.7 mile and then turn right at the Wapehani Mountain Bike Park sign. Follow the gravel road to the parking area.

Contact   Bloomington Parks & Recreation   812-349-3700

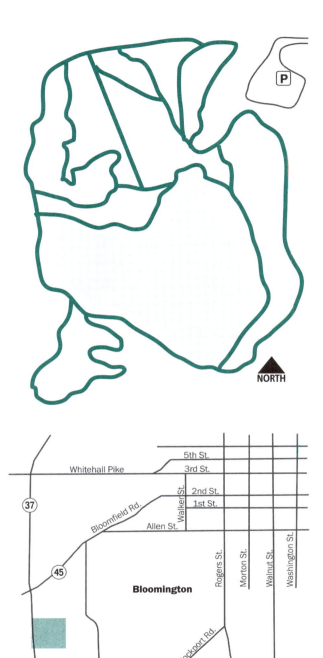

Yellow Banks Recreation Area

Trail Uses   🏍 🚶 ATV's

Vicinity   Dale, Selvin

Trail Length   4.5 mile loop, plus several miles of alternate trails

Surface   Singletrack, doubletrack, gravel road

County   DuBois

Trail Notes   The main trail loop circles Yellow Banks Lake, but the many alternate trails available frequently crisscross each other, making it difficult to keep track of where you are without paying attention to the keynote markers. Effort level is moderate and the setting is woods and fields. The trail has some decent climbs, and plenty of roots and ruts.

The Yellow Banks Recreation Area is like a mini-resort, with a fair number of daily activities. These include restrooms, showers, swimming, fishing, cabins, camping, pottery shops, picnic area, shelters, concessions, a grocery store, and scheduled craft shows. This is private property, and there is a small entrance fee.

Getting There   From I-64 east of Evansville between Hwy 61 and Hwy 231, take Hwy 161 South to Hwy 68. From there, turn right (west) and go north approximately 0.7 miles to the Yellow Banks Recreation Area entrance on the left side. The trails start just past the lakes dam to the left.

Contact   Yellow Banks Recreation Center   812-667-4703

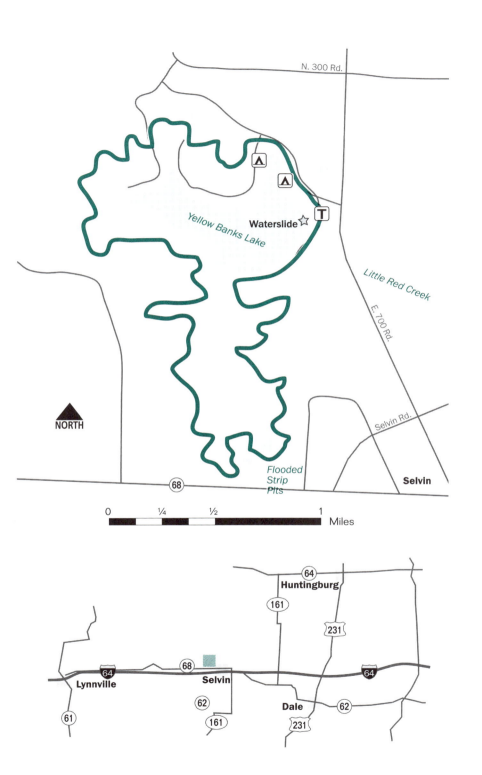

Youngs Creek Trail

Trail Uses	🏍 🚶 🐴
Vicinity	Paoli
Trail Length	10.5 miles
Surface	Singletrack, gravel roads
County	Orange

Trail Notes   Effort level for this trail system is difficult, and it is probably the most strenuous trail in Indiana. This shady trail traverses a variety of terrain in scenic hardwood forest. There are several challenging climbs and technical singletrack. Riding the trail clockwise may be a little easier, but either direction has rough climbs, fast downhills, mudholes, rutted horse tracks, protruding bushes, rocks and some logs to jump. You'll get some breaks on the gravel roads that appear at intervals along the route. The trail begins by the north end of the parking area. There are two climbs in the first mile and a half, followed by sharp descents down to a creek bed.

Facilities include a primitive campground with pit toilets, and a picnic shelter. Bring your own water and food. Mountain bikers and horse riders are required to have a trail permit, either daily or annual. Permits are available from Hoosier National Forest offices and local vendors.

Getting There   From Hwy 37, south of Paoli, to the Campground and the northern trailhead. Take Hwy 37, to CR 250 South, and proceed 0.9 miles to a brown FS sign. Turn left onto 50 West and follow it to the camp 1.2 miles on the left side of the road.

From Hwy 37 to the smaller trailhead. From Hwy 37 turn onto CR 550 South at the Pine Valley Store and proceed 0.8 miles to the Young's Creek trailhead on the right side of the road.

Contact   Tell City Ranger District   812-547-7051

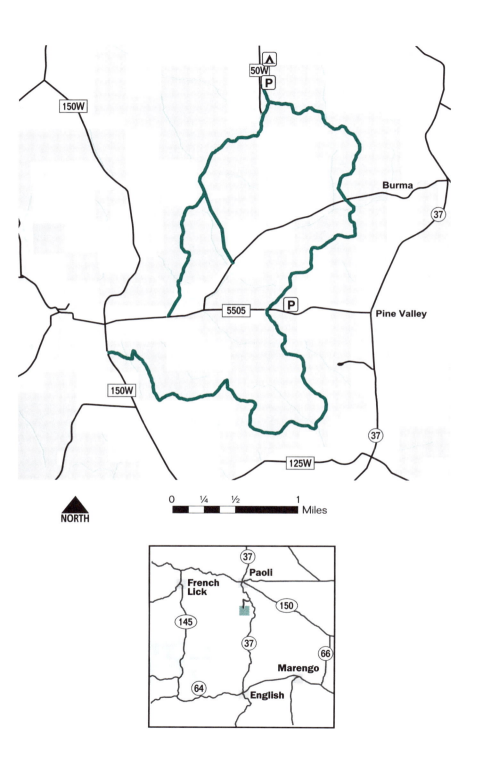

Photograph courtesy of Hoosier National Forest

Photograph courtesy of Hoosier National Forest

Explanation of Symbols

SYMBOL LEGEND	
🏖	Beach/Swimming
🚲	Bicycle Repair
🏠	Cabin
▲	Camping
🛶	Canoe Launch
✚	First Aid
🍴	Food
GC	Golf Course
?	Information
🛏	Lodging
MF	Multi-Facilities
P	Parking
🎪	Picnic
👤	Ranger Station
🚻	Restrooms
🏠	Shelter
T	Trailhead
🏛	Visitor/Nature Center
🚰	Water
🔭	Overlook/Observation

TRAIL LEGEND	
▬▬▬▬▬	Bike/Multi Trail
• • • • • • •	Hiking only Trail
▪▪▪▪▪▪▪	XC Skiing only
= = = = = =	Planned Trail
- - - - - -	Alternate Trail
▬▬▬▬▬	Road/Highway
┼┼┼┼┼┼┼	Railroad Tracks

AREA LEGEND	
	City, Town
	Parks, Preserves
▢	Waterway
	Marsh/Wetland
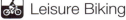	Mileage Scale
★	Points of Interest
- - -	County/State
🌲	Forest/Woods

TRAIL USES LEGEND	
🚴	Leisure Biking
🚵	Mountain Biking
🚶	Hiking
⛷	Cross-country Skiing
🐎	Horseback Riding
🛼	Rollerblading
🛷	Other

Selected Kentucky Trails

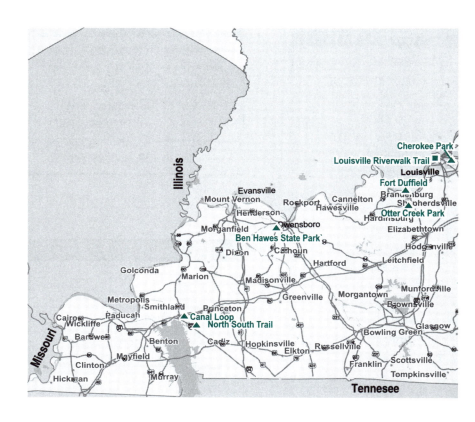

Trail Name	Page No.
Ben Hawes State Park	152
Briar Hill (Oldham County Park)	154
Canal Loop	156
Capital View Trails	158
Cherokee Park	160
Fort Duffield	162

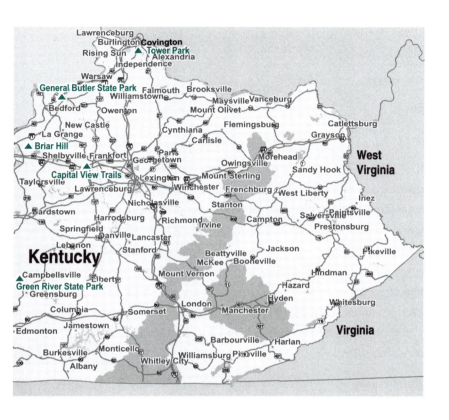

Trail Name	Page No.
General Butler State Park	164
Green River State Park	166
Louisville Riverwalk Trail	168
North South Trail	172
Otter Creek Park	174
Tower Park	176

Ben Hawes State Park

Trail Uses	🚵 🚶
Vicinity	Owensboro
Trail Length	10 miles
Surface	Singletrack, doubletrack, log roads
County	Davies

Trail Notes Ben Hawes State Park is densely wooded and sits on the remains of a deep coal mine operation that closed in the 1950's. Several buildings remain that can be reached from the trails. The trails vary from easy riding log roads, to moderate doubletrack to difficult tight and twisty singletrack. You'll find logs and roots thrown in for good measure. There are about 5 miles of logging road and doubletrack and 5 miles of singletrack. The out-and-back singletrack begins at Sara Gray's Loop and is marked with ribbon and way markers. Facilities at the park include a large golf course, shelters, picnic area and playgrounds. Spring is the time to enjoy the wildflowers throughout the northern end of the park.

Getting There From Owensboro take Hwy 60 West past the Ben Hawes main entrance on Booth Field Road. Continue west on Hwy 60 to Overstreet Road. The parking lot and trailhead is located at the abandoned George Rudy Mines and Saw Mill.

Contact Ben Hawes State Park 270-687-7134

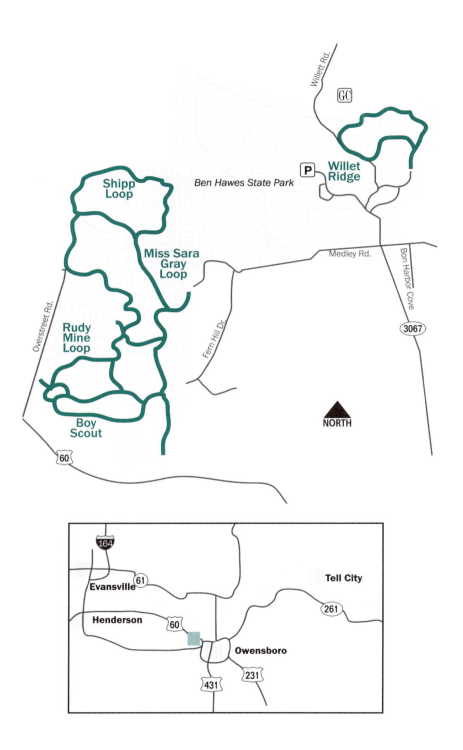

Briar Hill (Oldham County Park)

Trail Uses	
Vicinity	Louisville, Crestwood
Trail Length	8 miles
Surface	Singletrack, some paved road
County	Oldham

Trail Notes Briar Hill is a 56 acre county park. The trail system was developed as singletrack with an emphasis on technical riding. Effort level is moderate. The climbs and descents are short but intense, and will provide a challenge for the novice. The trails are twisty with numerous tight switchbacks, creek crossings, log jumps, bridges, and rocky drops. There is a cut through wooden bridge connecting the two sides of the trail. Close to this bridge is a steep drop off into a creek bed. Facilities are located by the parking lot and include drinking water, toilets, picnic table, and shelters.

Getting There Briar Hills is located two miles east of the city of Crestwood. From Gene Synder I-265 East, take Hwy 22 east for 4.5 miles and turn north on Briar Hill Parkway. The Parkway takes you to the parking area.

Contact Louisville Bicycle Club
www.louisvillebicycleclub.org

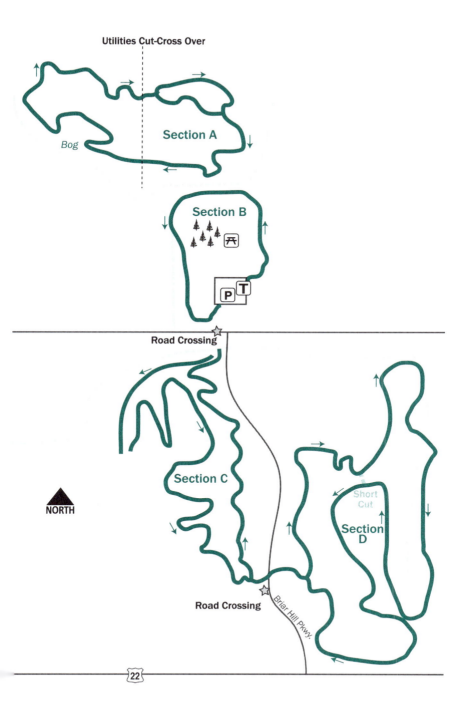

Canal Loop

Trail Uses	🚵 🚶
Vicinity	Paducah, Cadiz
Trail Length	14 miles
Surface	Single Trail, some fire road
County	Lyon

Trail Notes The Canal Loop Trail is a 14 miles multiple-use loop trail system, including four connector trails, and is located in the Land Between the Lakes recreation area. It can be accessed from either the North Welcome Station Trailhead or the Kentucky Lake Drive Trail Access. Effort level is easy to moderate. The trail is well maintained and marked by blue metal strips, while the connector trails are marked with yellow metal strips. The North/South Trail connects with the Canal Loop Trail at the North Welcome Station. The terrain is rocky with rolling hills and some short steep climbs. The ride will provide impressive views of Kentucky and Barkley Lakes. The surface generally stays dry. Bathrooms and drinking water are available, but you should treat trail-side water. Camping is available at Hillman Ferry Campground and Piney Campground.

Getting There From Paducah, go east on I-24 and take Exit 31 to Hwy 453 south towards Grand River. Cross the canal between Kentucky Lake and Lake Barkley and continue for 4.5 miles to Land Between the Lakes. The road becomes The Trace where you will arrive at the North Welcome Station.

Contact Tennessee Valley Authority   502-924-5602

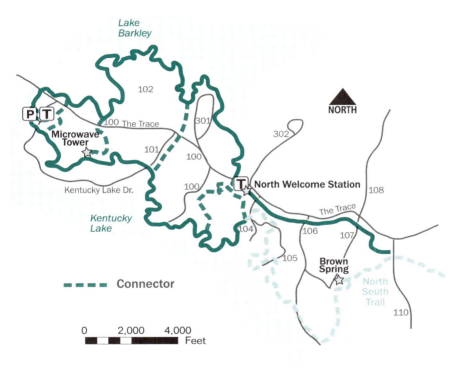

Capital View Trails

Trail Uses

Vicinity Frankfort

Trail Length 10 miles

Surface Singletrack, some doubletrack

County Franklin

Trail Notes The trails in this 150 acre park are mostly rolling singletrack, along with one doubletrack running through the entire network. They are generally smooth and fast with some challenging climbs. Effort level is easy to moderate, with some areas that should be of interest to more advanced riders. The first section is the Creek Loop, which zigzags down the creek and back up again. The second section is the Sinkhole Loop, which dives in and out of a couple of large sinkholes. The third section is the River Trail, which takes you along the Kentucky River with its scenic views. Park facilities include bathrooms and picnic areas. The park is open from 8:00 am to 11:00 pm.

Getting There From Louisville, take I-64 to Hwy 127. Turn left on Hwy 127, then right on the East-West connector, crossing the Kentucky River to Glenn's Creek Road. Take a left and then left again into the park. Follow the park road to the right to get to the parking area.

From Lexington, take I-64 to Hwy 60, then left on the East-West connector. Turn right on Glenn's Creek Road and then an immediate left into the park. Follow the road to the right to the parking area.

Contact Frankfort Parks & Recreation 502-875-8575

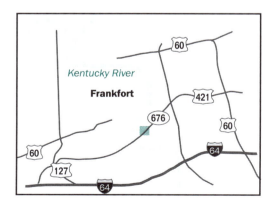

Cherokee Park

Trail Uses	
Vicinity	Louisville
Trail Length	12 miles
Surface	Singletrack with some paved road
County	Jefferson

Trail Notes   Cherokee Park opened in 1892 from land that was originally part of a 4,000 acre military land grant in 1773. The trailhead starts at Big Rock and bicycles are only allowed on trails on the north side of the creek. This is a loop with many small sections. There are some good climbs and downhills, with roots, rocks and even man-made obstacles in more technical areas. One area has a cliff bordering a creek with a very narrow singletrack running within inches of a steep drop down into this rocky creek. The trails can be quite muddy after a rain.

Getting There   From Taylorville Road, take Peewee Reese Road to the stop sign at Seneca Park Road. Turn left onto Seneca Park Road and take it to a stop sign. Across from the stop sign are Big Rock and a parking area. You can also turn left and park on the other side of the creek. Another of the many entrances to the park is off Alta Vista Road near the Presbyterian Seminary.

Contact   Olmsted Parks   502-456-8125

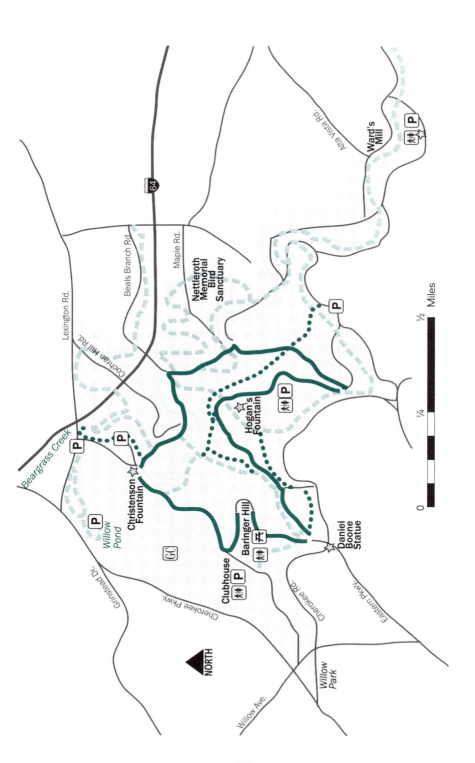

Fort Duffield

Trail Uses	
Vicinity	West Point
Trail Length	10 miles
Surface	Singletrack & some paved road
County	Hardin

Trail Notes This is the largest civil war fort in Kentucky, with great views of West Point and the Ohio River. The trail system is mostly singletrack with downhills, climbs, and several creek and log crossings. Effort level is moderate to difficult. From the parking lot the 300 foot paved climb goes up to where the main gate used to be. The trails start at the bottom of the old fort and are well marked with colored trail indicators painted on trees. Once behind the fort, the ride is tight and fast. There are several sections with steep dropoffs and cliffs so caution is warranted. Most of the ride is under forest canopy. Bring plenty of drinking water.

The Red Loop is about 5 miles long and a good starting point, with some good elevation change.

The Blue Loop starts off with a steep uphill switchback, mostly technical, and about 3 miles long.

The Downhill course is not for beginners, so be careful. It includes some small jumps.

The Giant Slalom course is fast and twisty. It's a long ride up and a very fast, short ride down.

Getting There From Louisville head south on US 31 W to West Point. When you see a large sign, turn into the park. Once in the park, take a right at the split in the road to a parking lot with trail access.

Contact   Fort Duffield   502-922-4674

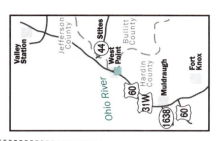
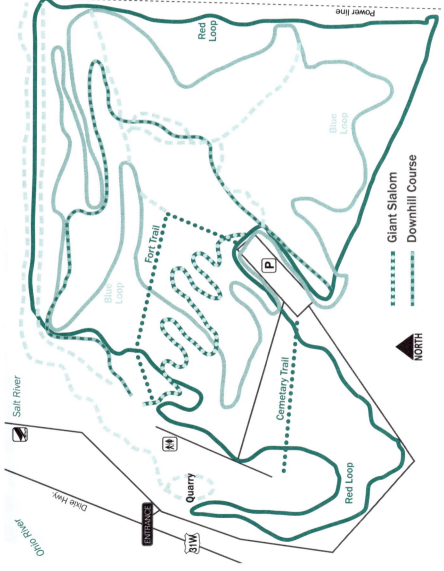

General Butler State Park (Fossil Trail)

Trail Uses

Vicinity   Carrollton

Trail Length   5.4 miles

Surface   Natural

County   Carroll

Trail Notes   This 791 acre resort park derives its name from General William Orlando Butler of revolutionary war fame. The 5.4 mile Fossil Trail loop crosses and follows open field areas, which are remnants of the closed Ski Butler slopes, and through old hardwood forests behind the Stone Overlook. The overlook is the highest elevation point in Carroll County, and is the perfect place to see the confluence of the Kentucky and Ohio Rivers. There are directional markers. Effort level is easy to somewhat moderate. The trails can become very slippery after rain. Helmets are required and no children under 16 years of age are allowed unless accompanied by an adult.

Facilities at the park include a lodge, cottages, campground, golf, marina, pool, picnic area, nature center, and recreation programs.

Getting There   The resort is located 44 miles northeast of Louisville. From Louisville, take I-71 to Carrollton. Hwy 227 takes you to the park entrance. You can access the trail from the back of the paved parking area on the left as you pass through the stone gates entering Stone Overlook Drive, or from the parking lot near the General Butler Conference Center

Contact   General Butler State Park   502-732-4384

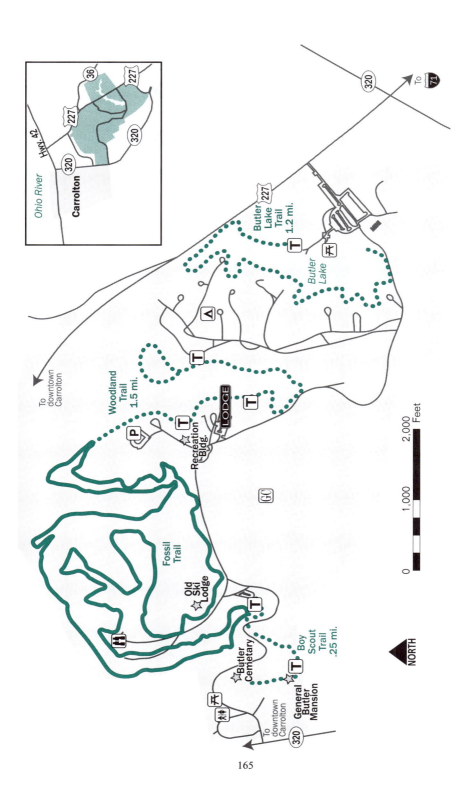

Green River State Park

Trail Uses	
Vicinity	Louisville, Campbellsville
Trail Length	20 miles
Surface	Mostly singletrack, some doubletrack
County	Adair, Taylor

Trail Notes   The trails vary from easy, to challenging, fast and technical. They are well maintained, with some shifting rock on short, steep climbs. Effort level is easy to moderate. You have a choice of several singletrack trails based on your technical skills. There are 6 main loops and several alternates as bypasses.

The Windy Ridge Loop is about a 4.4 mile ride taking you above the campground and lake. It begins just off the parking area, and then parallels the park road as it heads toward the beach. From the beach the trail continues to parallel the road and then the shore as it heads north, finally heading back to the parking area. There is also a short trail that spurs off to the right and heads down to the campground.

The North Loop is 5.4 miles long on the northern side of the park. It begins across the road near the parking area. Expect a number of twists and turns. One of the spurs is the Overlook Trail, providing some scenic views before looping back to its starting point.

The Marina Loop is 6.5 miles long, and starts at the west end parking area. It heads towards the park office, but continues on the trail until it splits. Take the trail to the right, and head towards the Green River Marina, then take a left to continue the loop. At the Y split, bear right to get back to the parking area.

The South Point Loop is 2.3 miles long, and starts in the parking area. It heads towards the water before returning to your starting point.

Getting There   From Louisville, go south on I-65 to Hwy 210. Take Hwy 210 east towards Campbellsville. Just past Campbellsville take Hwy 55 South to

Green River State Park. The entrance to the park is off 1061. Follow the main road towards the campground, passing the spur road to the park offices, and continue to a parking area on your right.

Contact   Green River State Park   270-465-8255

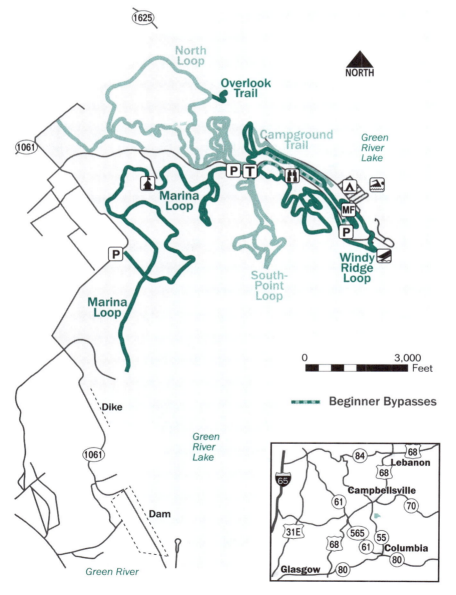

Louisville Riverwalk Trail

Trail Uses	
Vicinity	Louisville
Trail Length	12 miles
Surface	Paved
County	Jefferson

Trail Notes   This scenic multi-use path along the Ohio River is made up of two segments of about 6 miles each. The two segments are connected by a designated bike lane. There is also a 0.4 asphalt greenway path rail trail to the northeast of the north 6-mile segment. There are numerous bike lanes throughout Louisville, contributing to the city being designated a Bronze Bicycle Friendly Community by the League of American Bicyclists in 2006.

Getting There   Louisville is located south of the Ohio River, separating Kentucky from the state of Indiana.

Suggested trail parking and entrances: West Broadway at Shawnee Park. The road dead-ends into a parking lot, with the trail just around the bend to the left at the entrance to the park adjacent to the parking lot.

Take 21st/22nd Street to Northwestern Parkway - park at Lannan Park (turn right on N. 27th Street from Northwestern Parkway onto Lannan Park Road into the parking area), or park on-street further on Northwestern Parkway.

Waterfront Park – any of the park parking lots.

Contact   Louisville Bicycle & Pedestrian Coordinator
502-574-0104

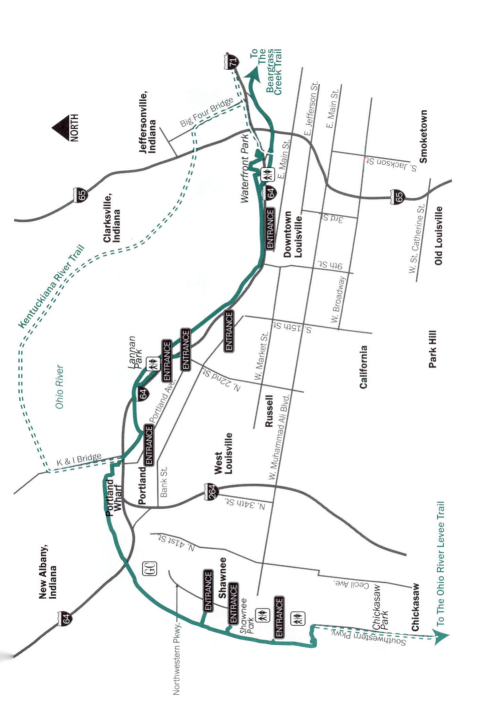

Louisville Riverwalk by Shawnee Golf Course

Photos courtesy of the Louisville Metro Bicycle & Pedestrian Coordinator

Mill Creek Bridge

North South Trail

Trail Uses	
Vicinity	Paducah
Trail Length	31 miles
Surface	Singletrack, logging & gravel roads
County	Lyon

Trail Notes The North South Trail connects the North Welcome Station with the Golden Pond Visitor Center. It provides a wide variety of terrain, traversing ridge tops, bottomlands, and the shoreline of Kentucky Lake. Effort level is easy to moderate. You can use this trail in conjunction with Land Between the Lake's authorized roads to form a series of shorter loops. You can also consider connecting to the Canal Loop Trail for a total of 45 miles. There is water available at the Hatchery Hollow halfway point, but bring your own as well, plus some power bars. Some have suggested starting at Golden Pond from the south and working your way to the North Welcome Station to get the worst of the hills and climbs behind you.

Getting There The Land Between the Lakes lies between Barkley Lake and Kentucky Lake. The North Welcome Station is located off 'The Trace' road and south of Hwy 62/641. The Golden Pond Visitor Center to the south is located just south of Hwy 68 and west of 'The Trace' Road.

Contact   Land Between the Lake   270-924-2000

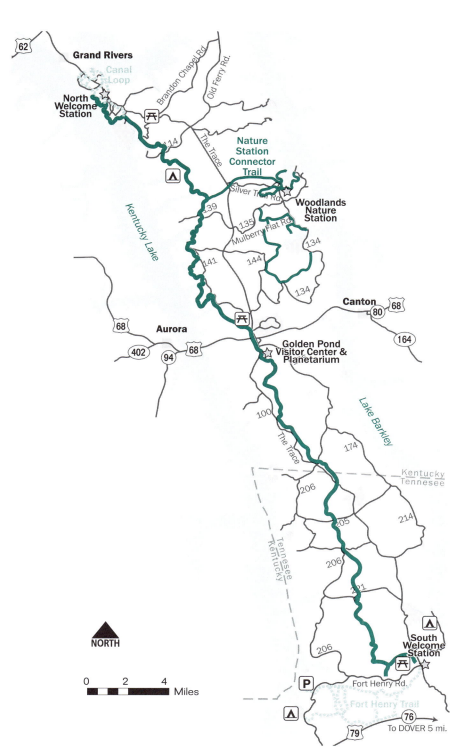

Otter Creek Park

Trail Uses	🚵 🚶 🎧
Vicinity	Muldraugh
Trail Length	20 miles
Surface	Singletrack, paved road
County	Meade

Trail Notes The park's namesake, Otter Creek, winds along the eastern side of the park. A scenic bend in the Ohio River, which divides Kentucky from Indiana, can be seen from northern overlooks within the park. Otter Creek's 2,600 acres provides the cyclist rolling sections of singletrack and fast downhills. Some of the trails are long and steep. Wood bridges and paved road are interspersed among the trails. Effort level varies from easy to difficult.

The Otter Creek Trail is an 8.1 mile loop around the perimeter of the park, with spur trails to such places as Morgan's Cave, the Ohio River, and Hughes Landing. This trail can get technically difficult with drop-offs and climbs.

The Red Cedar Trail is a 7.0 mile trail that meanders through the interior section of the park. Trail intersections are marked with signage.

The Valley Overlook Trail is a 3.9 mile loop through the uplands of the park, where you will experience some great views of the Otter Creek Valley. The trails are maintained by a local mountain bike organization.

Getting There Otter Creek is located west of Muldraugh and southwest of Louisville. From Louisville take the Dixie Hwy (31-W) south past the town of West Point to Muldraugh. Take a right on Hwy 1638 for about 3 miles and turn right on the entrance road for the park.

Contact Otter Creek Park   502-574-4583

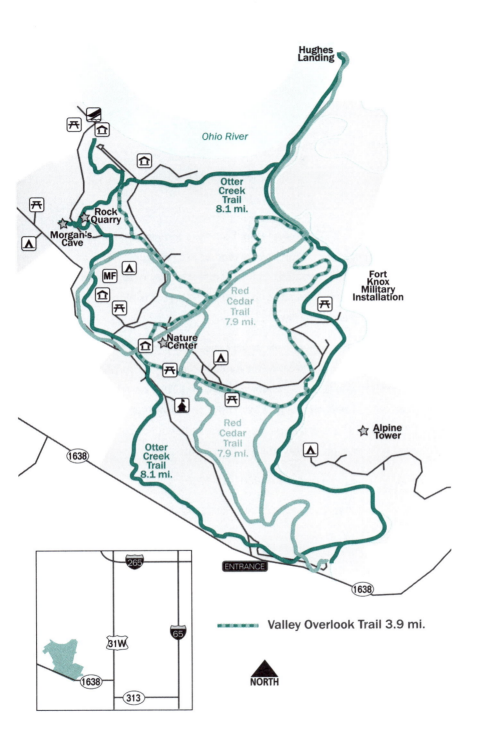

Tower Park

Trail Uses	
Vicinity	Covington, Fort Thomas
Trail Length	6 miles
Surface	Singletrack, fire & gravel road
County	Campbell

Trail Notes The Tower Park trail is predominately singletrack, with plenty of roots and rocks. Effort level is moderate to difficult. There are a couple descent climbs that are very tight and technical. One set of trails lead you down near the Ohio River and then back up again. The trail runs along a creek in some sections and is mostly flat.

Getting There Tower Park is only about ten minutes from downtown Cincinnati. Take I-471 South from Cincinnati to the Hwy 27 exit. Turn left onto Hwy 27, then left onto Grandview Avenue. At Fort Thomas Avenue turn left again (this is at a 4-way stop sign). Turn right on Tower Place and follow the signs to the park. There is a large stone tower at the entrance. The trailheads are located a various points towards the back of the park.

Contact Tower Park 859-781-1700

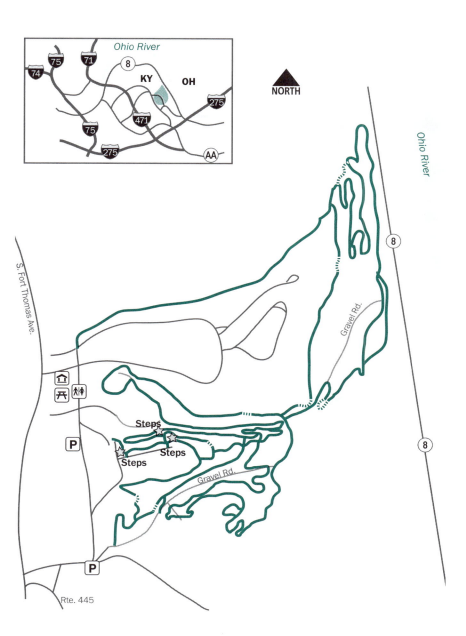

Trail Index

Trail Name *Page No.*

INDIANA

Trail	Page
Birdseye Trail	96
B-Line Trail	98
Bloomington Rail-Trail	98
Bluhm Property (Gust Trails)	20
Bonneyville Mill County Park	22
Brown County State Park	102
Calumet Trail	46
Cardinal Greenway	66
Central Canal Towpath	68
Clark State Forest	104
Clear Creek Rail-Trail	98
Delphi Historic Trails	70
Eagle Creek Trail	72
East Race Riverwalk	24
Erie Lackawanna Trail Linear Park	40
Fall Creek Trail	74
Ferdinand State Forest	106
France Park	26
German Ridge Recreation Area	108
Gnaw Bone Camp	110
Hickory Ridge Recreation Area	112
Iron Horse Heritage Trail	38
J.B. Franke Park	28
Jackson Creek Trail	98
Jackson-Washington State Forest	116
Kekionga Mountain Bike Trail	30
Lake City Greenway	32
Lick Creek	118
Linton Conservation Club	120
Martin State Forest	122
Mogan Ridge MTB Trails	124
Monon Trail & Monon Greenway	76
Nebo Ridge Trail	126
Nickel Plate Trail	34
Oak Savannah Trail	42
Ogala Trail	128
Oriole Trails	131

Trail Name	Page No.
Outback Trail	48
Owen-Putnam State Forest	80
Ox Bow Outer Loop Trail	50
Pennsy Greenway	38
Pleasant Run Trail	82
Pogues Run Trail	84
Prairie Duneland Trail	44
Pumpkinvine Nature Trail	52
Rivergreenway Trail	54
Rum Village Pathway	58
Shirley Creek, West Loop	134
Springs Valley Trail	136
Starve Hollow State Rec Area	138
Sugar Creek Community Trail	86
Tipsaw Lake	140
Town Run Trail Park	88
Veteran's Memorial Bikeway	39
Wapehani Mountain Bike Park	142
Westwood Park	90
White River Wahahain Trail	92
Winona Lake Trail	60
Yellow Banks Recreation Center	144
Youngs Creek Trail	146

KENTUCKY

Ben Hawes State Park	152
Briar Hill (Oldham County Park)	154
Canal Loop	156
Capital View Trails	158
Cherokee Park	160
Fort Duffield	162
General Butler State Park	164
Green River State Park	166
Louisville's Riverwalk Trail	168
North South Trail	172
Otter Creek Park	174
Tower Park	176

Surfaced Trails

Trail Name   *Page No.*

INDIANA

Trail Name	Page
B-Line Trail	98
Bloomington Rail-Trail	98
Calumet Trail	46
Cardinal Greenway	66
Central Canal Towpath	68
Delphi Historic Trails	70
Eagle Creek Trail	72
East Race Riverwalk	24
Erie Lackawanna Trail Linear Park	40
Fall Creek Trail	74
Jackson Creek Trail	98
Lake City Greenway	32
Monon Trail & Monon Greenway	76
Nickel Plate Trail	34
Oak Savannah Trail	42
Ox Bow Outer Loop Trail	50
Pennsy Greenway	38
Pleasant Run Trail	82
Pogues Run Trail	84
Prairie Duneland Trail	44
Pumpkinvine Nature Trail	52
Rivergreenway Trail	54
Sugar Creek Community Trail	86
Veteran's Memorial Bikeway	39
White River Wahahain Trail	92

KENTUCKY

Trail Name	Page
Louisville's Riverwalk Trail	168

Mountain Bike Trails

Trail Name *Page No.*

INDIANA

Birdseye Trail	96
Bluhm Property (Gust Trails)	20
Bonneyville Mill County Park	22
Brown County State Park	102
Clark State Forest	104
Clear Creek Rail-Trail	98
Delphi Historic Trails	70
Ferdinand State Forest	106
France Park	26
German Ridge Recreation Area	108
Gnaw Bone Camp	110
Hickory Ridge Recreation Area	112
Iron Horse Heritage Trail	38
J.B. Franke Park	28
Jackson-Washington State Forest	116
Kekionga Mountain Bike Trail	30
Lick Creek	118
Linton Conservation Club	120
Martin State Forest	122
Mogan Ridge MTB Trails	124
Nebo Ridge Trail	126
Nickel Plate Trail	34
Ogala Trail	128
Oriole Trails	131
Outback Trail	48
Owen-Putnam State Forest	80
Ox Bow Outer Loop Trail	50
Rum Village Pathway	58
Shirley Creek, West Loop	134
Springs Valley Trail	136
Starve Hollow State Rec Area	138

continued on next page

Mountain Bike Trails (continued)

Trail Name *Page No.*

INDIANA (continued)

Tipsaw Lake 140

Town Run Trail Park 88

Wapehani Mountain Bike Park 142

Westwood Park 90

Winona Lake Trail 60

Yellow Banks Recreation Center 144

Youngs Creek Trail 146

KENTUCKY

Ben Hawes State Park 152

Briar Hill (Oldham County Park) 154

Canal Loop 156

Capital View Trails 158

Cherokee Park 160

Fort Duffield 162

General Butler State Park 164

Green River State Park 166

North South Trail 172

Otter Creek Park 174

Tower Park 176

POPULATION CODES	② 1,000 to 5,000	④ 10,000 to 50,000
① Up to 1,000	③ 5,000 to 10,000	⑤ Over 50,000

City to Trail Index

City Name *Population* *Trail Name* *Page No.*

INDIANA

City	Pop	Trail	Page
Birdseye	❶	Birdseye Trail	96
Bloomington	❺	B-Line Trail	98
Bloomington	❺	Brown County State Park	102
Bloomington	❺	Jackson Creek Trail	98
Bloomington	❺	Hickory Ridge Recreation Area	112
Bloomington	❺	Wapehani Mountain Bike Park	142
Bloomington	❺	Bloomington Rail-Trail	98
Bloomington	❺	Clear Creek Rail-Trail	98
Bristol	❷	Bonneyville Mill County Park	22
Brownstown	❷	Starve Hollow State Rec Area	138
Brownstown	❷	Jackson-Washington State Forest	116
Burns Harbor	❶	Calumet Trail	46
Carmel	❹	Monon Trail & Monon Greenway	76
Chesterton	❸	Calumet Trail	46
Chesterton	❸	Prairie Duneland Trail	44
Crawfordsville	❹	Sugar Creek Community Trail	86
Crown Point	❹	Veteran's Memorial Bikeway	39
Crown Point	❹	Pennsy Greenway	38
Crown Point	❹	Erie Lackawanna Trail Linear Park	40
Dale	❷	Yellow Banks Recreation Center	144
Delphi	❷	Delphi Historic Trails	70
Derby	❶	German Ridge Recreation Area	108
Derby	❶	Mogan Ridge MTB Trails	124
Elkhart	❹	Ox Bow Outer Loop Trail	50
Ferdinand	❷	Ferdinand State Forest	106
Fort Wayne	❺	J.B. Franke Park	28
Fort Wayne	❺	Rivergreenway Trail	54
Freetown	❶	Ogala Trail	128
French Lick	❷	Springs Valley Trail	136
French Lick	❷	Shirley Creek, West Loop	134
Gary	❺	Oak Savannah Trail	42
Gaston	❶	Cardinal Greenway	66
Gnaw Bone	❶	Gnaw Bone Camp	110
Goshen	❹	Ox Bow Outer Loop Trail	50
Goshen	❹	Pumpkinvine Nature Trail	52
Griffith	❹	Oak Savannah Trail	42

continued on next page

City to Trail Index (continued)

City Name *Population* *Trail Name* *Page No.*

INDIANA (continued)

City Name	Pop.	Trail Name	Page
Griffith	❹	Erie Lackawanna Trail Linear Park	40
Highland	❹	Erie Lackawanna Trail Linear Park	40
Hobart	❹	Oak Savannah Trail	42
Huntington	❶	Kekionga Mountain Bike Trail	30
Indianapolis	❺	Pleasant Run Trail	82
Indianapolis	❺	Pogues Run Trail	84
Indianapolis	❺	White River Wahahain Trail	92
Indianapolis	❺	Eagle Creek Trail	72
Indianapolis	❺	Fall Creek Trail	74
Indianapolis	❺	Monon Trail & Monon Greenway	76
Indianapolis	❺	Central Canal Towpath	68
Indianapolis	❺	Town Run Trail Park	88
Jasper	❹	Ferdinand State Forest	106
Kokomo	❹	Nickel Plate Trail	34
Linton	❷	Linton Conservation Club	120
Logansport	❹	France Park	26
Lynnville	❶	Yellow Banks Recreation Center	144
Marengo	❶	Birdseye Trail	96
Medford	❶	Cardinal Greenway	66
Michigan City	❹	Calumet Trail	46
Middlebury	❷	Pumpkinvine Nature Trail	52
Monticello	❸	France Park	26
Muncie	❺	Cardinal Greenway	66
Munster	❹	Pennsy Greenway	38
Nashville, IN	❶	Brown County State Park	102
Nashville, IN	❶	Gnaw Bone Camp	110
New Castle	❹	Westwood Park	90
New Pekin	❶	Clark State Forest	104
Norman Station	❶	Hickory Ridge Recreation Area	112
Orleans	❷	Shirley Creek, West Loop	134
Paoli	❷	Lick Creek	118
Paoli	❷	Youngs Creek Trail	146
Paoli	❷	Springs Valley Trail	136
Portage	❹	Outback Trail	48
Portage	❹	Iron Horse Heritage Trail	38
Porter	❷	Prairie Duneland Trail	44
Rochester	❸	Nickel Plate Trail	34

City Name	Population	Trail Name	Page No.

INDIANA (continued)

City	Pop.	Trail	Page
Schereville	❹	Erie Lackawanna Trail Linear Park	40
Sellersburg	❷	Clark State Forest	104
Selvin	❶	Yellow Banks Recreation Center	144
Shipshewana	❶	Pumpkinvine Nature Trail	52
Shoals	❶	Martin State Forest	122
South Bend	❺	East Race Riverwalk	24
South Bend	❺	Rum Village Pathway	58
Spencer	❷	Owen-Putnam State Forest	80
St. Croix	❶	Tipsaw Lake	140
Story	❶	Nebo Ridge Trail	126
Sulphur	❶	Oriole Trails	131
Tell City	❸	Tipsaw Lake	140
Tell City	❸	Mogan Ridge MTB Trails	124
Tell City	❸	German Ridge Recreation Area	108
Warsaw	❹	Lake City Greenway	32
Warsaw	❹	Winona Lake Trail	60
Westville	❸	Bluhm Property (Gust Trails)	20

KENTUCKY

City	Pop.	Trail	Page
Cadiz	❷	Canal Loop	156
Campbellsville	❸	Green River State Park	166
Carrollton	❷	General Butler State Park	164
Covington	❹	Tower Park	176
Crestwood	❷	Briar Hill (Oldham County Park)	154
Fort Thomas	❹	Tower Park	176
Frankfort	❹	Capital View Trails	158
Louisville	❺	Cherokee Park	160
Louisville	❺	Briar Hill (Oldham County Park)	154
Louisville	❺	Green River State Park	166
Louisville	❺	Louisville's Riverwalk Trail	168
Maldraugh	❶	Otter Creek Park	174
Owensboro	❺	Ben Hawes State Park	152
Padauch	❹	North South Trail	172
Paducah	❹	Canal Loop	156
West Point	❷	Fort Duffield	162

County to Trail Index

County Name	Trail Name	Page No.
INDIANA		
Allen	Rivergreenway Trail	54
Allen	J.B. Franke Park	28
Brown	Brown County State Park	102
Brown	Nebo Ridge Trail	126
Brown	Gnaw Bone Camp	110
Carroll	Delphi Historic Trails	70
Cass	France Park	26
Clark	Clark State Forest	104
Delaware	Cardinal Greenway	66
Dubois	Ferdinand State Forest	106
DuBois	Yellow Banks Recreation Center	144
Elkhart	Pumpkinvine Nature Trail	52
Elkhart	Bonneyville Mill County Park	22
Elkhart	Ox Bow Outer Loop Trail	50
Fulton	Nickel Plate Trail	34
Greene	Linton Conservation Club	120
Hamilton	Monon Trail & Monon Greenway	76
Henry	Westwood Park	90
Howard	Nickel Plate Trail	34
Hungington	Kekionga Mountain Bike Trail	30
Jackson	Jackson-Washington State Forest	116
Jackson	Starve Hollow State Rec Area	138
Jackson	Hickory Ridge Recreation Area	112
Jackson	Ogala Trail	128
Kosciusko	Winona Lake Trail	60
Kosciusko	Lake City Greenway	32
Lagrange	Pumpkinvine Nature Trail	52
Lake	Oak Savannah Trail	42
Lake	Erie Lackawanna Trail Linear Park	40
Lake	Pennsy Greenway	38
Lake	Veteran's Memorial Bikeway	39
Lake	Prairie Duneland Trail	44
LaPorte	Bluhm Property (Gust Trails)	20
Marion	Central Canal Towpath	68
Marion	Pogues Run Trail	84
Marion	Monon Trail & Monon Greenway	76
Marion	Town Run Trail Park	88
Marion	Pleasant Run Trail	82
Marion	White River Wahahain Trail	92
Marion	Fall Creek Trail	74
Marion	Eagle Creek Trail	72
Martin	Martin State Forest	122

County Name	Trail Name	Page No.
INDIANA (continued)		
Miami	Nickel Plate Trail	34
Monroe	B-Line Trail	98
Monroe	Jackson Creek Trail	98
Monroe	Bloomington Rail-Trail	98
Monroe	Wapehani Mountain Bike Park	142
Monroe	Clear Creek Rail-Trail	98
Montgomery	Sugar Creek Community Trail	86
Orange	Springs Valley Trail	136
Orange	Shirley Creek, West Loop	134
Orange	Lick Creek	118
Orange	Birdseye Trail	96
Orange	Youngs Creek Trail	146
Owen	Owen-Putnam State Forest	80
Perry	Mogan Ridge MTB Trails	124
Perry	German Ridge Recreation Area	108
Perry	Tipsaw Lake	140
Perry	Oriole Trails	131
Porter	Prairie Duneland Trail	44
Porter	Iron Horse Heritage Trail	38
Porter	Calumet Trail	46
Porter	Oak Savannah Trail	42
Portor	Outback Trail	48
Putnam	Owen-Putnam State Forest	80
St. Joseph	East Race Riverwalk	24
St. Joseph	Rum Village Pathway	58
Washington	Jackson-Washington State Forest	116
KENTUCKY		
Adair	Green River State Park	166
Campbell	Tower Park	176
Carroll	General Butler State Park	164
Davies	Ben Hawes State Park	152
Franklin	Capital View Trails	158
Hardin	Fort Duffield	162
Jefferson	Louisville's Riverwalk Trail	168
Jefferson	Cherokee Park	160
Lyon	North South Trail	172
Lyon	Canal Loop	156
Meade	Otter Creek Park	174
Oldham	Briar Hill (Oldham County Park)	154

Bicycle Components & Tips

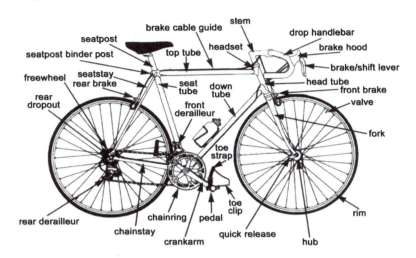

Tires and Wheels
Inspect your tire's thread for embedded objects, such a glass, and remove to avoid potential punctures.
Carry with you a spare tube, a patch kit, tire levers for removing the tire, and some duct tape.
Don't reassemble the wheel when fixing a flat until you have felt around the inside the tire. The cause of the puncture could still be lodged there.
Adjust your tire inflation pressure based on the type of ride. Lower pressure is better for off road biking or riding in the rain. A higher tire pressure is best for normal road biking or racing.
Sometimes a clicking sound is caused by two spokes rubbing together. Try a little oil on the spokes where they cross.

Reflectors
Have at least a rear reflector on your bike. Reflectors on the back of your pedals is an effective way of alerting motorists' to your presence.

Pedals
A few drops of oil to the cleat where it contacts the pedal will help silence those clicks and creaks in clipless pedals.

Saddles
Replace an uncomfortable saddle with one that contains gel or extra-dense foam. Select a saddle best designed for your anatomy. Women generally have a wider distance than men between their bones that contact the saddle top.

Chains and Derailleurs
Avoid combining the largest rear cog with the large chainring or the smallest cog with the small chainring.
Noises from the crank area may mean the chain is rubbing the front derailleur. To quiet this noise, move the front derailleur lever enough to center the chain through the cage but not cause a shift.

Find me a place, safe and serene,

away from the terror I see on the screen.

A place where my soul can find some peace,

away from the stress and the pressures released.

A corridor of green not far from my home

for fresh air and exercise, quiet will roam.

Summer has smells that tickle my nose

and fall has the leaves that crunch under my toes.

Beware, comes a person we pass in a while

with a wave and hello and a wide friendly smile.

Recreation trails are the place to be,

to find that safe haven of peace and serenity.

By Beverly Moore, Illinois Trails Conservancy

American Bike Trails publishes and distributes maps, books and guides for the bicyclist. For these and other book and map selections visit our website.

American Bike Trails
www.abtrails.com